ALISON LYSSA writes plays, poetry, short fiction and essays. *Pinball* owes much to the Women and Theatre Project which Chris Westwood and Jude Kuring initiated in 1980 to redress the dire lack of opportunities for women in Sydney's theatres. The reading of *Pinball*, directed by Fay Mokotow at Nimrod Theatre, Sydney, led to productions there and at Troupe, Adelaide (1981).

In 1998, Debra Hely directed *Pinball* for Newcastle Repertory, NSW, and a reading was staged at the International Theatre Conference: 'From Sappho to the Third Millennium: Homosexuality in Mythology, Religions and Plays', Lesbos, Greece. Duck Duck Goose Theatre performed *Pinball* at the Tap Gallery, Darlinghurst, for Sydney's Mardi Gras, February 2014, directed by Sarah Vickery.

Alison's play *The Boiling Frog* (1984) premiered at Nimrod Theatre, Sydney, and has also been performed in Adelaide, SA; Cygnet, Tas.; Wagga Wagga, NSW; and, Canberra, ACT. Alison's *Who'd've Thought?* (1990) created with the Women's Theatre Project, Telopea, NSW, was nominated for an AWGIE (1991). In 1992, aided by an interpreter, Joyce Chiu, Alison helped the Cantonese–speaking Careforce Women's Theatre Group, Cabramatta, NSW, to write and perform their bilingual play, *What can a mother do?*

Alison's study at the Australian Film Television and Radio School led to the filming of her short screenplay, *The Silk*, adapted from Joy Cowley's short story. *The Silk* received an Australian Film Industry nomination for Best Screenplay in a Short Film (1994), and won an ATOM Award (1995).

Alison has taught Writing for Performance and Creative Writing at the University of Technology, Sydney, the University of Western Sydney, and Macquarie University, where she gained her Masters for a thesis entitled 'Performing Australia's Black and White History' (2006), and her PhD for a study called 'Terror on Stage', which includes an original playscript, *Hurricane Eye: A Masque for the Twenty-first Century* (2014).

Kerry Walker as Vandelope in the 1981 Nimrod Theatre production.

PINBALL
Alison Lyssa

CURRENCY PRESS
The performing arts publisher

CURRENCY PLAYS

First published in Australia in 1996 in
Australian Gay and Lesbian Plays
by Currency Press Pty Ltd,
PO Box 2287, Strawberry Hills, NSW, 2012, Australia
enquiries@currency.com.au
www.currency.com.au

This edition published 2021.

Copyright © Alison Lyssa, 1996, 2021.

COPYING FOR EDUCATIONAL PURPOSES

The Australian *Copyright Act 1968* (Act) allows a maximum of one chapter or 10% of this book, whichever is the greater, to be copied by any educational institution for its educational purposes provided that that educational institution (or the body that administers it) has given a remuneration notice to Copyright Agency (CA) under the Act.

For details of the CA licence for educational institutions contact CA, 11/66 Goulburn Street, Sydney, NSW, 2000; tel: within Australia 1800 066 844 toll free; outside Australia 61 2 9394 7600; fax: 61 2 9394 7601; email: info@copyright.com.au

COPYING FOR OTHER PURPOSES

Except as permitted under the Act, for example a fair dealing for the purposes of study, research, criticism or review, no part of this book may be reproduced, stored in a retrieval system, or transmitted in any form or by any means without prior written permission. All enquiries should be made to the publisher at the address above.

Any performance or public reading of *Pinball* is forbidden unless a licence has been received from the author or the author's agent. The purchase of this book in no way gives the purchaser the right to perform the play in public, whether by means of a staged production or a reading. All applications for public performance should be addressed to the author c/- Currency Press.

Lyrics to the song *Don't be too Polite, Girls*, are copyright © 1985 Glen Tomasetti.

Cover design by Lisa White.

Currency Press acknowledges the Traditional Owners of the Country on which we live and work. We pay our respects to all Aboriginal and Torres Strait Islander Elders, past and present.

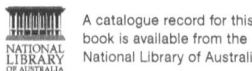

A catalogue record for this book is available from the National Library of Australia

AUTHOR'S NOTE

> Lesbians possess a sexuality which is by definition active and actively out of the control of men, therefore requiring the heightened scrutiny of the courts.
> ... When lesbians try to keep custody of their children through the courts they face a wealth of prejudices relating to single mothers, lesbians, female sexuality and the construction of motherhood in this society.
> ... discrimination against lesbians in custody cases is tied to a continuum of scrutiny regarding women's sexuality and as such lesbian custody is an issue for all women.
> ... Values are revealed in the use of language by the judges, reflecting disgust at active female sexuality, presumptions of disease or mental illness, lesbianism as a general defect, and heterosexuality as normal and preferable.
> Jenny Milbank, 'Lesbian Custody: a Feminist Issue'
Polemic 2.3 (1991), pp.142–145.

When I wrote *Pinball* in 1980, bashing it out on an old typewriter, I would never have supposed that in 1996 I'd be going into the State Library of New South Wales, keying 'lesbian custody' into a brilliant CD-Rom search facility and discovering instantly that the struggle was still going on. Women are still facing judges who make the presumption that a lesbian parent is likely to be harmful to a child.

I agree with Jenny Milbank that the judges' scrutiny of lesbians has implications for all women. In *Pinball*, Theenie is engaged in a struggle not only to hold on to her right to nurture and love her child, but also to construct a world where she can hold onto and nurture herself. Her powerful opponents do not want to hear the questions she keeps asking. Each in their own way, her father, her brother and Solomon regard her search for her own truth as so dangerous, they draw on centuries of tradition to control the very language that she uses. They try to use her love for her child to make her conform to their precepts. When she refuses, they fight to force her compliance so they can control the destiny of future generations.

Unlike Cordelia in *King Lear*, Theenie does not allow herself to be taken captive and hanged. Whereas Cordelia is alienated from her sisters and isolated from all other women, Theenie is able to draw on the support of Axis and Vandelope. They remind her that to discover herself she has to take risks and challenge the powerful prejudices that want to destroy her.

Many critics at the time were scathing of my play, accusing me of a biased and distorted view of the world. All these years later Jenny Milbank's article reminds me that unfortunately I did not pull the character of Solomon out of nowhere. A number of his outrageously anti-women comments came from actual court transcripts. Many judges today still seem to fear women's self-determination. At the end of the play Solomon is horrified when he realises the women have resisted him effectively and that power is slipping from him.

When I wrote *Pinball* I hoped it would not only present my ideas and tell a story, but entertain as well. I'm excited that the play is continuing to have a life, and want to thank again all the people who gave their advice and support in its creation.

Alison Lyssa
Sydney, 1996

To the memory of Fay Mokotow 1946–1984 and many others who have died too young.

Kerry Walker as Miriam in the 1981 Nimrod Theatre production.

The Women and Theatre Project gave *Pinball* a workshop and a public reading in February 1981, directed by Fay Mokotow.

Pinball was first performed by the Nimrod Theatre Company in the Downstairs Theatre, Sydney, on 9 September 1981 with the following cast:

THEENIE	Jenny Ludlam
AXIS	Natalie Bate
VANDELOPE/ MIRIAM	Kerry Walker
LOUISE/ VIOLET	Cecily Polson
SYLVESTER/ ARCHIBALD	Roger Leach
SOLOMON/ KURT/ WAITER/ SERGEANT/ HOTEL GUEST	Paul Bertram

Director, Chris Johnson
Designer, Kate Jason Smith
Lighting designer, Kevin McKie
Sound effects, Michael Carlos
Stage manager, Stephanie Walkem

CHARACTERS

THEENIE, artist and mother of Alabastar
AXIS, Theenie's partner
VANDELOPE, anarcho-lesbian bicyclist
SYLVESTER, Theenie's ex-husband
LOUISE, Sylvester's wife
VIOLET, Theenie's mother
ARCHIBALD, Theenie's father
KURT, Theenie's brother, and Solomon's alter ego
MIRIAM, Kurt's wife
SOLOMON, a biblical figure
WAITER, SERGEANT, HOTEL GUEST, Solomon's alter egos

The play is intended to be performed by six actors. ALABASTAR remains invisible. The company contribute the CROWD's offstage voices.

SETTING

Non-naturalistic and fun. Bare stage. Lighting creates atmosphere, for example: a stained glass effect for Solomon's Bible reading and the Christening; flickering lights for the pinball parlour; a green light for the billiard room; a sweep of car headlights and a whirling blue police light for the outdoor scene at night where the women graffiti the wall. A table starts life as a pinball machine, and converts as needed to other purposes, for example, as restaurant or billiard table.

Pinball is also published in:

Michelene Wandor (ed.) *Plays by Women*, Vol IV., (London: Methuen, 1985) 119-159.

PROLOGUE

Pinball machines lit. Electronic firing. Organ music to suit Old Testament drowns pinball machines. Pinball machines go out. Stained glass window lit.

SOLOMON *enters wearing biblical robes.*

SOLOMON: [*reading from 1 Kings 3, v 9–28*] '… and God said to Solomon … "Behold I give you a wise and discerning mind, so that none like you has been before you and none like you shall arise after you. I give you also what you have not asked, both riches and honour …"

'And Solomon awoke and behold, it was a dream …

'Then two harlots came to the king … The one woman said, "Oh, my lord, this woman and I dwell in the same house; and I gave birth to a child … Then on the third day after I was delivered, this woman also gave birth; and we were alone; there was no one else with us in the house; only we two were in the house. And this woman's son died in the night, because she lay on it. And she arose at midnight and took my son from beside me … and laid it in her bosom, and laid her dead son in my bosom. When I rose in the morning to nurse my child, behold it was dead, but when I looked at it closely in the morning, behold it was not the child that I had borne." But the other woman said, "No, the living child is mine and the dead child is yours."

'Then the king said, "Bring me a sword." So a sword was brought before the king, and the king said, "Divide the living child in two, and give half to the one, and half to the other."'

Organ music. ALABASTAR's *voice, making a sound of firing, builds up to a sound battle with the organ music. The organ music, defeated, fades. Stained glass window fades. Blackout.*

ACT ONE

SCENE ONE

Pinball parlour. VANDELOPE *enters. Sound of pinball machines.*

SOLOMON: The child, Alabastar, here in a pinball parlour?

He introduces himself to the audience.

Solomon's the name.

He looks with disdain at a machine.

Caveman's the game? Sometimes one needs an audience while collecting evidence. Thirteen boys, three girls and you have to look in the dictionary before you know what that one is.

VANDELOPE: Piss off!

She plays a video game.

Jeep! Blll! Loooop!

She makes electronic firing noises.

Score two hundred!

SOLOMON: I prefer the old-fashioned kind with flippers. One can see where the balls go.

VANDELOPE [*making firing noises*] Bluumm! Tank! You beauty. Score five hundred! Brrip! United Nations truck.

She swears.

Soya beans. Lose three seconds.

SOLOMON 'And the voice of the turtle dove
Is heard in our land.'

VANDELOPE: Ooops, Vandelope, there goes El Salvador.

SOLOMON: This is the space age. Why aren't they home playing cowboys and indians like we did?

VANDELOPE: They send kids here to school. Teaches them how to talk to coloured lights bipping, face to face.

SOLOMON: Where is the boy? He must be somebody's son.
Madam! I'm looking for the owner of a son.
VANDELOPE: I'm not into that. I'm an anarcho-lesbian bicyclist.
SOLOMON: He was last seen with a pile of coins, asking for a cigarette, and he must be all of ten.
VANDELOPE: See if he'll lend me twenty cents.
SOLOMON: This little boy has potential.
VANDELOPE: If men had to give birth to children they'd pop out of their skulls just like that—fully clothed and brainwashed, drooling 'Come to where the flavour is.'
SOLOMON: You women have gone out to work, and a whole generation suffers from neglect.
VANDELOPE: You know why I wear overalls? So when a jerk like you pops out at me, I can put my arms in here and give myself a cuddle.
SOLOMON: 'I compare you, my love
To a mare of Pharaoh's chariots.'
VANDELOPE: Get knackered. Give him an inch and he thinks he's Ben Hur.
SOLOMON: I'll remember that.
VANDELOPE: I come here to get away from it and the patriarchy follows me. It thinks I'm an addict.

She checks her pockets.

Destitute!
You know they're making a fortune out of you, so you have another game to take your mind off it. Pigs. I was going to hang onto enough for a thickshake.

She pulls down a sign with graffiti on it: 'THE RICH COME HERE TO FORGET, THE POOR TO DREAM.' She goes out.

SOLOMON: Bring in the harlots,
I'll judge who's his mother.
Sharpen my sword,
I've already won …
Only a harlot would cut up a son.

He sees what Vandelope has done.

Concubine! Vandal!
VANDELOPE: [*off*] Yep!
SOLOMON: I'll catch her later. Now there are more important visitors.

SCENE TWO

SOLOMON *conjures the pinball machine into a table. Uses his biblical robe to make a formal tablecloth, revealing him dressed as an elegant* WAITER. *He discovers that the cloth has graffiti on it: 'EAT THE RICH'. He hastily turns the cloth over. Adds two chairs. An expensive menu. Lights out on pinball machines.*

WAITER: 'He brought me to the banqueting house,
    And his banner over me was love.'

    LOUISE *enters with a thick folder of notes.*

Madam, table for one?
LOUISE: Two. Three.

    She sits.

Merci. A perfectly easy restaurant. They can't possibly be late. I wonder if ten-year-olds like steak without chips. It's going to be a big responsibility. Someone's life to organise. I want to give the boy the choice that leads men up.
WAITER: She is the perfect flower who married the father yesterday.

    SYLVESTER *arrives and gives* LOUISE *a kiss.*

SYLVESTER: Louise, darling.
LOUISE: Darling.
SYLVESTER: Sorry I'm late, Professor Sinclair wanted to see me.
LOUISE: I've put your notes together for you.

    She hands him the notes.

I've added a piece on Althusser, picking up the themes of collaboration and resistance.
SYLVESTER: Darling, that's wonderful. The Prof was delighted with the first draft. He's given me a pat on the back.

LOUISE: Darling.
SYLVESTER: You've been such a support. I should put your name on it, as co-author.
LOUISE: No, darling, I couldn't do that.
SYLVESTER: Yes, we could, darling.
LOUISE: No, really, darling, I couldn't. It's yours.
SYLVESTER: We're so happy together. Shall we start with the terrine?
WAITER: 'Eat, O friends, and drink:
   Drink deeply, O lovers!'
LOUISE: Mmm. Darling, weren't we going to do this with Alabastar?
SYLVESTER: Darling, could you persuade him to have quail in orange brandy when he's walking past 'Big Mac' in neon lights?
LOUISE: You left him there? For lunch? To do what he wants? Darling, you don't know who might be there.
SYLVESTER: Louise, darling, relax. They do the garlic prawns beautifully here.
WAITER: Garlic prawn.
SYLVESTER: Alabastar would be bumping the table leg every time you and I looked at one another.
WAITER: Take your time, sir.
LOUISE: I love it when we're perfect together.
WAITER: Rack of lamb, Madam?
   'Your cheeks are like halves of a pomegranate
   Behind your veil.'
LOUISE: I do so want to get on well with Alabastar.
SYLVESTER: I want you to think of him as ours.
LOUISE: After lunch, should we take him to the museum? The art gallery? Sylvester darling? You have organised the afternoon free?
SYLVESTER: Mmm. Yes, darling. The art gallery, no. Perhaps the fish soup?
WAITER: *Bouillabaisse*.
LOUISE: Mmmmm. Do you think he could do with some shopping, now we've got him in town? New jeans? A cricket bat?

SYLVESTER: He wants a Space Invaders machine—to take home.
LOUISE: That's ridiculous. I mean, that can't be good for him.
SYLVESTER: I had to promise it to him, darling. It's been difficult for him, for both of us. Please understand.
LOUISE: Darling, if he's going to spend puberty with a pinball machine, you ought to book him into a decent school.

>*The* WAITER *covers the graffiti sign with chalkboard menu: 'SPECIALS OF THE DAY'.*

SYLVESTER: We can't move fast, my darling. Theenie won't let us. I know she won't. Louise, I love you. Louise, Theenie wouldn't just make an issue out of it, she'd make a revolution.
LOUISE: Let her keep her ugly old sandshoes and struggles, but if she goes on dragging Alabastar into them, he'll never learn how to sit down to dinner in the right company. She's not his mother any more. She is his ex.
SYLVESTER: My ex, darling. Would you prefer the Balmain bugs *au beurre*? He's happy and learning at Edgebank Public. Plenty of his friends will be going on to the local high school. It's not as though we live in an unsavoury area.
LOUISE: I'm rather taken by the rainbow trout. Be reasonable, darling. I've seen how it hurts you when people ask what school you went to and you have to answer Cardigan Boys High.
SYLVESTER: That was while I was fighting for a lectureship. Now that next semester I've been offered the Marxist Studies Course, it's good that I've had exposure to the mixed lens of humanity. You know what those students are into. Anything that flies in the face of convention. Consciousness raising. Food co-ops. I can't send Alabastar to a private school. Student assessment of lecturer: nil.
LOUISE: But remember how you suffered. How you lost that tooth for reading *Pride and Prejudice* in the playground. Do you know what my favourite, is, dearest? Avocado vinaigrette.
WAITER: Avocado vinaigrette.

>*He goes.*

SYLVESTER: Superb. Louise, don't you see? I can bite on that capped tooth and remember. When you were at school, didn't you feel that life had breadth?

LOUISE: Darling, it was enriching at Lamington Ladies College: hockey, front row, Byron, Chapel at eight, Michelangelo, the annual GPS Regatta and *Oedipus Rex*. We must get Alabastar off to a good start.

SYLVESTER: We have.

LOUISE: If we can get the tomato sauce off his tee shirt.

    WAITER *re-enters with table napkins.*

WAITER: 'As an apple tree among the trees of the wood,
    So is my beloved among young men.'

SYLVESTER: You're growing to love him, aren't you? The shoulders on him!

WAITER: 'His neck is like the tower of David
    Built for an arsenal.'

    He goes.

SYLVESTER: He's more Theenie's build than mine.

LOUISE: Sylvester, let's not think of her any more, darling. The point is, we can afford the fees, he's probably scholarship material anyway, and he needs a private school as an antidote to that woman.

SYLVESTER: Theenie is not *that* woman. And don't worry about Alabastar. Theenie's done the groundwork—Vitamin B, books from Dr Seuss and a set of Scrabble on his seventh birthday. He'll make it whatever school we send him to.

LOUISE: She's a better mother by the minute. I don't know why you bothered to get a divorce.

SYLVESTER: Darling, I did it for you. I knew I loved you when I found myself looking forward to my lectures, because you'd be in the front row, sitting there with your folder open. You made me feel I had somewhere to belong.

LOUISE: It's all right for you. Wherever you go someone's going to make you belong there. Fifty percent of the time, you said, Alabastar's got to be with us fifty percent of the time. But how am I going to belong with you if Alabastar's hers?

SYLVESTER: Darling. Stop it! I can't bear that I've hurt you. I had no idea. Darling? I'll canvass my colleagues for the best of all possible schools.

The WAITER *re-enters.*

LOUISE: Sylvester. I can't bear us to quarrel. Darling, look, if his future's out of danger and he's set his heart on that video game, we could buy it, now, a present from both of us.

SYLVESTER: No, no, darling. From you! As your welcome to Alabastar.

LOUISE: Darling, I knew you could be tender and perceptive. *Garçon!* Where could we find the Space Invaders?

WAITER: 'How much better is your love than wine,
    And the fragrance of your oils than any spice!'

LOUISE: Where's the pinball department?

WAITER: On the mezzanine, Madam. Santa Claus is in Aladdin's cave, on the right as you come off the escalator.

> LOUISE *and* SYLVESTER *go out,* SYLVESTER *giving the* WAITER *a small tip on the way.*

WAITER: *Merde!* So well-dressed and so rude.
    'And when the Queen of Sheba
    Had seen all the wisdom of Solomon,
    The house that he had built,
    The food of his table,
    And his burnt offerings
    Which he offered at the house of the Lord,
    There was no more spirit in her.'
A good old lesson. Harlots! Take note. Now, does anybody else want a piece of this child?

> THEENIE *enters.*

SCENE THREE

WAITER *removes coat. Takes off tablecloth, puts on dirty apron. Covers chalkboard menu with Coca-Cola advertisement: 'SMILE, COKE ADDS LIFE'. Turns menu inside out. Now a cheap Lebanese restaurant.*

WAITER: [*during the above activities*]
    'King Solomon made himself a palanquin
    From the wood of Lebanon.
    He made its posts of silver,
    Its back of gold, its seat of purple:
    It was lovingly wrought within
    By the daughters of Jerusalem.'
You come up in the world, you come down in the world.

Lebanese music.

    'What is that coming up from the wilderness,
    Like a column of smoke,
    Perfumed with myrrh and frankincense?'

AXIS enters with a bicycle helmet, a luminous jacket and a smog mask.

AXIS: As I rose out of the evening peak
    Head down head choking
    Bicycle past news of sieges …

THEENIE: Sounds like where we live.

She embraces AXIS.

WAITER: Two of them! In all my born days.

He goes.

AXIS: Did you get anything done?

THEENIE: I've been standing in front of the canvas for hours, not painting, stabbing.

AXIS: Don't give up, Theenie. Anybody who tries to paint humanity with confidence is going to have days when nothing happens.

THEENIE: I'm sick of 'almost'. I want it magnificent. Have you seen the way Alabastar's hands move? Zap, zap, sideways, dodging, and it's on the screen that very instant, as if any second his life is going to blow up.

AXIS: If he's got twenty cents he gets another one.

THEENIE: I hate those machines. Why couldn't I work today? I get an idea, I try to do it …

Pause.

AXIS: Stop worrying about what other people are going to think.

THEENIE: I'm not good enough.

AXIS: You are. It's your palette and your brush. Go on, say it, 'I'm a painter and I'm good.'

THEENIE: I'm … I'm … Oh, Axis.

She hugs her.

Thanks. How was your day?

AXIS: Don't ask. I'll get onto the latest government cuts at the clinic.

THEENIE: Is that going to send you all into another collective depression?

AXIS: We're not going to let it. I've been doing pregnancy tests all day. When the last one came out positive I didn't know how to break the news to the woman; she looked like she'd fall apart. But she was thrilled. Been trying to have a kid for years.

THEENIE: Hooray.

WAITER: [*re-enters*] 'Your two breasts are like two fawns …'

AXIS: Two large mixed plates please.

WAITER: 'Twins of a gazelle

That feed among the lilies.'

AXIS: Hang on—one vegetarian.

WAITER: Vegetarian.

THEENIE: And if we could please, a carafe of white wine.

WAITER: White wine.

THEENIE: Almond cakes, coffee.

WAITER: Almond cakes, coffee.

THEENIE: Oh, and Turkish delight.

WAITER: Turkish delight.

He goes.

AXIS: Theenie, are we having a party?

THEENIE: A funeral for Western society. Sylvester's bought a Space Invaders console.

AXIS: For himself or his students?

THEENIE: For Alabastar.

AXIS: How are we going to afford to switch him on?
THEENIE: He's back with us tomorrow. It's our month.
AXIS: Hope you fixed it so we always get the short months.
THEENIE: I want to see him.

   Pause.

   When he's home with me I can't ever go into the studio and shut the door.
AXIS: Guilt.
THEENIE: Crap. When he's gone, it hurts, there's something missing.
AXIS: Yeah, dirty socks. I'll find something to turn him on. Do-it-yourself bread? Bicycle maintenance? Creative graffiti?
THEENIE: We spent hours with him making that billycart. He rode it down the hill once, and he was back inside demanding more money for the robot in the laundromat.
AXIS: Maybe we can save up to buy him a hang-glider. Sorry, Theenie. Every time we try to eat, try to get to know each other, in comes the update on Alabastar, and you plonk him in the middle of the bed … I mean the table.
THEENIE: He has learnt to knock.
AXIS: He's nearly ten.
THEENIE: When he was born they gave me bowls of peaches. They covered the end of the bed with blue forget-me-nots, pansies and shawls. Now they're teaching him to open fire.
AXIS: Well, you could have had a girl child.
THEENIE: Is that the only way you can think of making paradise?
AXIS: All I mean is, if you'd had a girl, it would be easier. She wouldn't be anybody's hero, she wouldn't have anything to inherit. You could take a girl with you to self-defence classes.
THEENIE: What the hell do you want? Keep a knife by the bedside in case one pops out, and then cut it off and tuck it in? Expose them on the hillside like they did with unwanted girls? It craps me off when people give up hope for Alabastar because he was born a boy. That's as senseless as blaming everything on Eve or Pandora.
AXIS: Calm down.

THEENIE: I won't have people telling me that evil comes because of that male piece of punctuation. If I have to believe that, I'm running out of here like Jocasta, to hang myself.
AXIS: Shut up. I want to get drunk. And I love you.
THEENIE: And Alabastar?
AXIS: Sometimes I think you don't see me.
THEENIE: Axis, let's get off this tightrope.
AXIS: I don't think we own the ground down there. Or the wire we're balancing on.
WAITER: [*entering with a basket of bread*]
'How graceful are your feet in sandals,
O queenly maiden.'

He leaves.

THEENIE: There's nothing we can do about it. My brother gave Alabastar a gun for Christmas. When we got home Vandelope was there.

Lights change.

Our friend the pacifist.
AXIS: In her jungle greens.

She plays a mock firing game with AXIS *and the invisible* ALABASTAR. VANDELOPE *enters.*

VANDELOPE: So this is Alabastar. I've met him. On the pinnies.

Firing video game noises.

He thinks he can bring a machine gun in here, does he? Good one. Boom. Got 'im.

Firing noises.

THEENIE: Alabastar dear. Put it away.
VANDELOPE: Away? Smash it. You know what little macho shits grow into. Big macho shits. As if having a gun cocked with bullets isn't enough, they grow their own, the fuckers. Put it down, Alabastar, I said, put it down. Only pigs and warmongers have guns—Stalin, Reagan, Pinochet and Alabastar. Aw Shulamith, now I've made him cry.
THEENIE: Don't cry, Albie. She didn't mean to jump on you.

AXIS: Go on, Vandelope. Explain to him that right now we have to fight our way out from under, but when the anger's all come out and changed the world we're gonna live in peace.

VANDELOPE: If you put your commitment to male children above your commitment to women …

AXIS: Heavy.

THEENIE: Albie, we'll get you a soccer ball.

VANDELOPE: If you put your commitment to male children above your commitment to women … Holy Germaine! Anybody coming? I've got a few billboards to bugger up.

She leaves.

THEENIE: Go if you want to, Axis, follow her. She's so lucky, so pure, she's never even had a tampon inside her.

AXIS: You don't have to send me away, Theenie.

They embrace. Lights change.

THEENIE: The sun's come out.

AXIS: Okay, Alabastar, let's go down the canal and play.

She plays a game with THEENIE *and the invisible* ALABASTAR. *Invisible ball!* VANDELOPE *enters. Writes graffiti on Coca-cola billboard: 'SMILE: WHILE U STILL GOT TEETH.' Then joins the ball game between* AXIS, THEENIE *and* ALABASTAR. *The* WAITER *re-enters and tries to join the game.*

WAITER: 'Catch us the foxes, the little foxes,
That spoil the vineyards,
For our vineyards are in blossom.'
[*Hit in the middle with the ball*] Ooof!

AXIS and THEENIE collide and embrace at the moment. VANDELOPE goes. The WAITER kicks it away.

Howzat.

He notices THEENIE *and* AXIS *kissing.*

Harlots! Break it up. You'll put the customers off their food.

THEENIE: Appeal to his rationality, Axis. His inbred sense of justice

AXIS: I'll phone Vandelope. She'll know a lawyer. Arrest this restaurant.

She kisses THEENIE.

WAITER: 'The juice of my pomegranates.' What a waste!

He separates AXIS *and* THEENIE.

AXIS: How come you're not molesting that couple of heterosexists up the back?

WAITER: They have a right to enjoy their evening in peace.

AXIS: Enjoy their evening? They're canoodling, paddling up to their necks, and because they're a man and a woman it'll turn up on children's TV.

THEENIE: Axis, don't. Let's go.

AXIS: I haven't eaten my dinner.

THEENIE: We can't fight the whole world.

AXIS: He's discriminating against women on the grounds of sex. Call the cops.

WAITER: Get out of here. You sluts are ruining my business.

AXIS: Stuff your business!

The WAITER *exits.*

THEENIE: Come home, Axis, come home.
The kettle calls on the stove;
The curtains keep out the cold.
The walls, the walls make us free.

AXIS: I want justice! Do I have to turn the tables over before I can have a quiet dinner? Lay my head on a woman's breast, and you insult me. Vandelope! Help! Slander! Ho! Police!

The WAITER *enters wearing a* SERGEANT's *coat and hat.*

WAITER: Behold, the paddy wagon!
'About it are sixty mighty men ...
All girt with swords
And expert in war ...
Each with his sword at his thigh.'

THEENIE: Axis, we can reason our way out of this.

AXIS: Good evening, officer, sir, would you be so helpful as to

register formal charges against this place of business and its manager for violating the Anti-Discrimination Act.
SERGEANT: You'll have to come down to the station.
AXIS: You don't understand. You have to book the restaurant.
SERGEANT: I've had dinner, love.
THEENIE: Axis, he's bigger than us.
AXIS: I'm not going to have him call me 'love'.
SERGEANT: [*seizing* AXIS] Come on, love.
THEENIE: You're hurting her. Police don't hurt people.
AXIS: You're breaking my arm, you dickwit.
THEENIE: Please stop.
SERGEANT: Are you coming quietly, lady, or head first and noisy?
AXIS: Let me go.
SERGEANT: Bloody communist drug-fiends!
AXIS: Radioactive mine owner from Queensland!

> THEENIE, AXIS *and the* SERGEANT *leave in disarray.* VANDELOPE *strolls through with a sandwich board, the front of which reads: 'SISTERS, KEEP A SMILE ON YOUR LIPS AND A SONG IN YOUR HEART', and on the back: 'WHILE YOU'RE SMASHING THE STATE'. She rearranges chairs for the next scene.*

VANDELOPE: [*singing*]
> Don't be too polite, girls
> Don't be too polite.
> Show a little fight, girls,
> Show a little fight.
> Don't be fearful of offending in case you get the sack,
> Just recognise your value, and you won't look back.
> All among the bull, girls,
> All among the bull …

She leaves. SOLOMON *enters.*

SOLOMON: Manhater! Hijacking harlot!

> VANDELOPE, *off, blows a raspberry.* SOLOMON *covers* VANDELOPE'*s coca-cola ad graffiti.*

Give them their heads and they'd change the scenery. I'm the one with the overall view.

He hangs up a banner: 'HAPPY BIRTHDAY ALABASTAR'.

The child is turning ten. Now's the time to infiltrate the party.

Changes his coat to become KURT.

Disguise myself as a plant in the heart of the nuclear family. The boy needs his uncle, Kurt, a capital man, of my own calibre. He'll know what the boy wants in a mother.

'I would lead you and bring you
Into the house of my mother,
And into the chamber of her that conceived me.'

He goes.

SCENE FOUR

VIOLET *enters during* KURT's *last speech, followed by* ARCHIBALD, *both wearing party hats, and carrying a punch bowl and a tray of punch cups. Light opera music, e.g. a Gilbert and Sullivan medley.*

VIOLET: The children can eat in the rumpus room, they'll be less of a mess and bother.

ARCHIBALD: Theenie rang to say she's bringing that woman.

VIOLET: We'll need another chair for the adults then, dear.

ARCHIBALD: My dear Violet! Must you encourage my daughter in that unspeakable house full of bandwagons? Last year a pro-communist war, this year women's lib, next month the Aborigines and any moment now they'll discover something useful, like rainforests.

VIOLET: Dearest, she believes in good causes. There but for the grace of God go you or I.

ARCHIBALD: I would not want her to be insensitive to injustice, but she embarrasses. Any excuse to demonstrate the disruption of our peace, from government bashing to graffiti, and our daughter is in attendance. Doesn't she realise our country is being handed over on a platter to the very bus-stop collection of union-mongers and liberationists who are plunging it into bankruptcy?

VIOLET: On your grandson's tenth birthday.

    THEENIE *and* AXIS *enter.*

THEENIE: Hello, Mum.

VIOLET: Hullo, Theenie.

THEENIE: Hullo, Dad. This is Axis. My parents. Violet and Archibald.

ARCHIBALD: How do you do, Axis? Axis. First names already. I'll save my protests.

    Pause.

VIOLET: Arch.

ARCHIBALD: Would you ladies like a party punch?

AXIS: Thanks.

THEENIE: Cheers!

VIOLET: Where's our Alabastar?

THEENIE: Hiding in the willows. He's a tree pirate.

ARCHIBALD: Pirate eh? [*Calling*] Alabastar? Here comes the big crocodile. [*To* THEENIE.] Remember? Coming to get you. Tick tock, tick, tock.

    He goes.

VIOLET: Be good to your father, won't you? He's feeling the strain of work. There's so little decency left in the world.

THEENIE: I'll be good. I care for you both, you know that.

    She hugs VIOLET.

VIOLET: That's my girl. [*To* AXIS] And you, dear, it's nice of you to come, it's nice of you to have each other, and be friends. [*To* THEENIE] Theen, anytime you want to invite her over for a meal, dear, just let me know, and it's nice for you and Alabastar, having an auntie in the house. Now I wonder where the others are? Come and we'll get out the good tea set, not much use saving it till I'm dead and gone. [*Leaving*] Arch! Alabastar!

THEENIE: Thanks for coming.

AXIS: Your old man wants to put me in the zoo.

VIOLET: [*off*] Come on, Theen.

THEENIE *goes.*

AXIS: Write me a message that I don't exist.

VIOLET *enters carrying a jug with more punch.*

VIOLET: Oh, dear, Alabastar does need a haircut, he can't possibly see out, dear. You have to find the wisdom to choose. The good Lord gave Theenie the brains to use, heaven knows.

AXIS: We were going to do it for him this morning. Only we had a bit of trouble finding the scissors in the chaos. Theenie's working on a new painting.

VIOLET: When she was little she loved bright colours. I'd get her those pots of fingerpaint and we were always running out of red.

AXIS: She still loves to rub her fingers in the paint.

VIOLET: One day she painted a whole story on the lounge-room wall. It's still there, under the wallpaper. And what do you do, dear?

AXIS: I see people. In a clinic. I get fed up with it sometimes.

VIOLET: Oh, you're a nurse, aren't you?

AXIS: Not exactly. We have …

ARCHIBALD *enters with a chair. There are now three chairs.*

VIOLET: Over there, dear. We'll need the cake tray down from the top shelf and a ribbon to tie on the knife.

She leaves.

AXIS: It's a beautiful old jug. Is it crystal?

ARCHIBALD: Young lady. You do appreciate … You have a responsibility to consider Alabastar.

AXIS: I do.

ARCHIBALD: It is important that you tell me what you think … of our landscape. An original.

AXIS: It's very nice.

ARCHIBALD: Ah! Do you dabble with the brush, too? Like our Theenie?

AXIS: Dabble? It's Theenie's work.

SOLOMON *enters as* KURT *with a bottle of brandy.*

KURT: Behold! A wise and kingly spirit.
ARCHIBALD: Son, how do you do?
KURT: How do you do, father?
ARCHIBALD: Napoleon, ah.
KURT: 'Who is this that looks forth like the dawn,
Fair as the moon, bright as the sun ...'

AXIS gives KURT a dirty look.

'... Terrible as an army with banners?'
ARCHIBALD: Allow me to introduce a relative newcomer to the family, currently establishing her reputation as an art critic. Kurt Havistock, may I present Miss Axis ... Axis mmm.
KURT: We've met. An art lover, eh? Did you have time to study the collection of Old Masters when you were at Central Court?
AXIS: I am outnumbered.

She leaves.

ARCHIBALD: What was she doing in court?
KURT: It would not be very loyal of me to tell you.
ARCHIBALD: Loyal?
KURT: To Theenie. She is entitled to her secrets.
ARCHIBALD: Kurt, we are a family. We have our name.
VIOLET: [*off*] Arch, dear, the ham. Are you ready with the carving knife?
ARCHIBALD: Now is neither the time nor the place, but this is no light matter, son.

He leaves.

MIRIAM: [*off*] Darling!

She enters, pregnant, bearing a pavlova pudding.

KURT: Christ!
MIRIAM: Darling, is there anything else to bring in out of the car? I do hope Sarah and Matthew behave themselves; it's boring when they don't.

AXIS enters with things for the table.

Hullo! Who's this?
AXIS: Well, I'm …
KURT: Theenie's latest.
MIRIAM: Beautiful hair. It does set off your head, short like that, but how long did you leave the henna in? [*To* KURT] She's actually beautiful, darling, what a waste!
AXIS: Don't turn away. Teach me how you wrap the sugar round the put-down.

> THEENIE *enters bearing a dish.*

THEENIE: Oh, my God. Don't take them on, Axis.
AXIS: I'm taking them off.

> VIOLET *enters.*

VIOLET: Don't upset your father, Theenie, Kurt. There's the worry of his kidneys.
AXIS: Truce.
VIOLET: [*calling*] Alabastar!

> *She takes the dish from* THEENIE.

Come on, darling, call the others. Children! Your frankfurters are ready in the rumpus room. Grandad's waiting.

> *She leaves.*

KURT: Give Miriam the comfortable chair.
  'The fig tree puts forth its figs,
  And the vines are in blossom.'
Would you like a cushion for your back?
MIRIAM: Please. Thank you, darling. Happy mummy, happy baby.

> VIOLET *enters.*

VIOLET: I didn't buy enough yo-yos. Isn't it funny how everybody wants one? Children, children. It takes two to make a quarrel.
THEENIE: Do sit down, Violet.

> AXIS *stands to give* VIOLET *her chair.* VIOLET *glares at Kurt who has remained seated.*

VIOLET: Theenie, what have you been up to, dear?
THEENIE: I've started a—

ARCHIBALD: [*entering from the rumpus room*] Little children should be seen and not heard.

THEENIE: Actually, I've—

ARCHIBALD: May I help anyone to a glass of liquid refreshment? Would you do the honours, son?

KURT: I think Theenie's about to tell us what she's been up to, Theenie?

He offers her a drink.

[*Calling*] I don't care who started it. Matthew, you hit your sister again and you can forget about football.

ARCHIBALD: I would venture to suggest without fear of contradiction that the behaviour of the children is the fault of our schools, where rampant left-wing influences exult in the subversion of discipline, diligence and decorum.

VIOLET: A growing boy needs his vitamins. I hope you're taking them every day now, Miriam.

KURT: Yes, mother, she is. Sarah! Let your mother have her rest.

MIRIAM: There's no need to take it out on the children. Sarah and Matthew are at very good schools. They have their altercations, naturally, but they adore one another.

She exits to the rumpus room.

VIOLET: [*to* ARCHIBALD] I'll have a drop more, thank you, dear. I wouldn't entirely blame the schools. There's more nonsense on television …

KURT: It's the Teachers' Federation, mother. I've told you that.

MIRIAM: [*re-entering with a child's stained white dress*] Sarah! Kurt, she wanted to wear her new white dress and now look! If you knew how it makes me tired.

She leaves with the dress.

KURT: [*to* ARCHIBALD] Don't fill Miriam's glass. She becomes uncontrollable. [*Shouting*] No more crisis-mongering in there, Sarah. I've told you not to cry. Don't cry. Okay? Just don't cry. [*To* VIOLET] I wouldn't put it past her to pull his hair.

AXIS: Theenie, you've got to say something.

THEENIE: Where would I start?

MIRIAM: [*returning*] My charming Mr Havistock senior, now that the children have promised to be good, may I?

She holds up her glass.

VIOLET: Miriam, you have your baby to think of.

KURT: She's drinking for two.

ARCHIBALD: For the blossoming Mrs Havistock junior, a pleasure.

VIOLET: Arch, dear, you haven't answered me. You always change the subject when what I say about television is right.

KURT: Mother, television is a powerful vehicle for freedom of choice, an indispensable part of the market, and of your financial destiny as an Australian shareholder.

VIOLET: We can have a destiny and a sense of responsibility.

MIRIAM: I consider television a godsend for the mother with a commitment to her husband's career.

VIOLET: Are the children ready for their chocolate crackles?

KURT: Just a minute, mother. No sweets for Matthew and Sarah until they've got every sandwich off their plate.

THEENIE: Aren't you being a bit savage, Kurt? You're piling so many rules in front of them they'll never see over the top.

MIRIAM: Waste not, want not. Think of the starving millions.

KURT: You might be my sister, but you mind your own bloody business.

VIOLET: Don't use language here, Kurt.

KURT: Yes mother, I'll swear in my father's house if I bloody well want to. [*To* THEENIE] How dare you criticise the upbringing of my children, when I suffer in silence the aberrations of you and your ill-trained offspring.

VIOLET: Theenie, a soft answer turneth away wrath.

THEENIE: It's okay, Violet. I don't want to quarrel.

THEENIE *gives her mother a kiss.*

ARCHIBALD: The disgrace is not the food, but the language. A generation is growing to adulthood with the grammar of the gutter. It comes this very afternoon from my grandson's mouth. 'I done whatcha said.' The greatest work of genius in the history of mankind is the English language. It catches at an old man's heart when the treasure house of centuries is ransacked.

THEENIE: No, Dad. It's changing, growing. If we did a Rip Van Winkle backwards for a hundred years, we'd find the language very different.

ARCHIBALD: That argument does not hold. I knew a time when it was the great men of letters who moved the language forward.

AXIS: And the women.

ARCHIBALD: I'll start again. I knew a time when it was the great men of letters—and history includes Jane Austen and George Eliot—who created our language and its beauty. Now it has become fashionable to adopt the speech and manners of the proletariat. The children of the least educated are dictating to us how we shall talk. 'I done whatcha said.'

VIOLET: [*perfectly modulated*] I did what you said.

ARCHIBALD: Thank you, Violet.

MIRIAM: I did enjoy the claret cup.

THEENIE: Are you sure it's a choice between I *done* and I *did*? I mean, once we used to say, 'I have done', then someone invented 'I've done', and now the adults are saying it so quickly, all the children hear is 'I done'. We're moving to a faster language, away from the restrictions of the apostrophe.

ARCHIBALD: My dear daughter! What we have lost in clarity and precision …

AXIS: Our Alabastar's helping. The other day he told me, 'I already undone them there knots meself, but'.

ARCHIBALD: Theenie, you must move.

VIOLET: Arch, dear, couldn't we manage somehow to send Alabastar to a private school?

AXIS: I don't think they'd like my sandshoes on parent-teacher nights.

THEENIE: Don't tease them, Axis, I can't bear it.

MIRIAM: Have you ever had the opportunity to have children, Axis, dear?

KURT: Are you being optimistic, or ridiculous? How can women's libbers have a sensible conversation about motherhood? Look in the media. They tirade against it. But notice how she says, 'Our Alabastar'. Mark my words, as soon as these women realise their control over the next generation is slipping out from under them, you'll see an immediate revival of the maternal instinct they've been so busy thwarting.

AXIS: Bullshit.

ARCHIBALD: I will not have the language of the tavern in my house.

AXIS: I'm sorry. But do give me a moment to defend myself.

KURT: Moment! I have an hour. Take the chair.

MIRIAM: Kurt.

AXIS: I can choose to give birth if I want to, and right now I've got other things to do. How come, when you can't have a baby yourself, you think you have a god-given right to tell me how to run my maternal instinct? You're not going to put me down.

KURT: Nobody put you up in the first place.

THEENIE: Axis.

MIRIAM: Go on, Axis, spit at him, like you did at the policeman in court. Oh! Sorry! Is it a secret?

VIOLET: Kurt, get your father his tablets.

AXIS: This is so fucking real, I'm getting out of here.

THEENIE: Wait. Please, Axis.

AXIS: I've got to apologise again, have I?

THEENIE: No. No. This time he has. Listen, Kurt, you may be my brother, and I used to love playing marbles with you, but I didn't come here for your judgement. I came because I love my warm-hearted mother and I love my dear old conservative dad, and we enjoy our odd conversations on language and the death of the King's English. And you can't turn Alabastar into a dog that you train how to bark, and you can't turn me into you. I'm going out to the kitchen to stuff myself on the biggest piece of pavlova since the Sydney Opera House. [*To* AXIS] Are you proud of me?

AXIS: Yep. For sanity's sake, let's go.

THEENIE: Yes. No. Everybody's ideology's at stake, but I can't leave before the birthday cake.

AXIS: I can smell the passionfruit and cream.

    AXIS *takes the pavlova.* THEENIE *and* AXIS *go out.*

MIRIAM: I need to do my yoga breathing to plan my reduced serving of pavlova.

She leaves.

KURT: Father, why have you allowed Theenie and that woman such a disgraceful exhibition?

VIOLET: Now, Kurt, Theenie's got an opportunity my generation didn't have to work it out for herself.

ARCHIBALD: Work it out? You expect me to welcome the female-involvement society? The multi-cultural society? Do you know what lies behind that balderdash? Every troublesome, unqualified, ungrammatical, pill popping dishmop of a housewife to be found in this country, and every guttural, lisping tinpot god of a migrant desperate to settle here, thinks he … or she, is entitled to the freedom to dictate to everybody else. Already at Havistock Credit we do our market research in sixteen languages and three sexes. And an upstart Turk comes into the office, the sort that hangs gold rings in the nose of half a dozen wives, devoid of any understanding of democracy, and dammit, he's an indispensable multi-national contact!

VIOLET: Arch, dear, your daughter's just like you, she cares.

ARCHIBALD: Yes, Violet, you are right. Our daughter is only a symptom, but she has a heart. She hasn't been left an easy life since that business of the divorce. Sylvester was a lovely boy. I'm worried about the polarisation, son. I'm worried that the decent people, the intelligent people, are going to be forced to build a high wall around their heritage, and patrol the boundaries with machine guns against the pillage of this vile generation. And that is not the freedom I have worked for in my life.

KURT: It will be Theenie's friends we'll have to shoot.

ARCHIBALD: That is harsh, my son.

VIOLET: It's no wonder there are wars.

    MIRIAM *enters.*

ARCHIBALD: My dear, sit down. Let your old father-in-law have a kind womanly smile.

    MIRIAM *smiles and takes* ARCHIBALD's *cup of punch.*

KURT: 'You have ravished my heart
    With a glance of your eyes.'

Look at her. Ready for another baby, and still Bo Derek.

MIRIAM: And look at him. My brilliant lawyer and judge-to-be. As wise as Solomon. She just dropped a willow pattern jug, your sister's wife.

VIOLET: I don't know why you all can't live and let live.

MIRIAM: Kurt, they're unnatural. Theenie kissed her. On the lips.

She puts her arms around KURT *for reassurance.*

KURT: Well? You could have said something.

MIRIAM: I walked out.

KURT: It's time you learned to present an intelligent argument. [*Calling*] Theenie! Axis!

MIRIAM: Don't bring them in here. I'm relaxing.

KURT: Don't give me instructions. Stand up for what you believe in.

MIRIAM: Darling, you're embarrassing me.

KURT: You're letting the side down. Challenge them or they'll have you in a factory like the women in Russia.

VIOLET: Arch, you marshal the children while we bring in the birthday surprise. Come along, Miriam, get your punch-bowl. And after that you must put your feet up.

VIOLET *and* MIRIAM *leave.*

ARCHIBALD: Now's the time, son.

KURT: Theenie and that woman were both in court like a couple of witches. On charges of indecent language, immoral acts in public, offensive behaviour, assaulting a police officer in the execution of his duty, malicious damage to the interior of a paddy wagon, and resisting arrest.

ARCHIBALD: Don't tell your mother.

KURT: Are you going to let her behave like that and keep custody? Do we sit by and lose a Havistock to the other side?

ARCHIBALD: Get me Sylvester's phone number. We'll save my grandchild if we have to take it to the highest court in the land.

ARCHIBALD *leaves.* VIOLET, MIRIAM, AXIS *and* THEENIE *enter,* THEENIE *carrying a birthday cake made like a pinball machine with ten candles lit.*

THEENIE: It's lovely, Violet.

Lights out.

ARCHIBALD: [*off*] Line up behind the birthday boy. Get your guns ready. Straight line. Wait for it. Quick march.

He enters with invisible children.

Left, right, left, right. Halt!

ALL: [*singing*] Happy birthday to you
Happy birthday to you
Happy birthday, dear Alabastar
Happy birthday to you.

ARCHIBALD: Hip hip …

ALL: Hooray.

VIOLET: Make a wish, Alabastar, make a wish.

Candles are blown out. They all go out in the dark, clearing props from the party scene, while singing:

ALL: For he's a jolly good fellow …

Etcetera.

SCENE FIVE

Plush old country hotel. Green light on the table. Imaginary billiard balls. AXIS *and* THEENIE *enter with billiard cues. Sound of billiard balls and pinball machines.*

AXIS: Lovely cut! I've got my eye in now.

She plays.

Blew it! Theen. Theenie!

THEENIE: What? What are you doing?

AXIS: I sunk four in a row.

She kisses THEENIE. SOLOMON *enters, disguised as a hotel* GUEST. *With billiard cue.*

AXIS: [*to* THEENIE] It's your turn.

GUEST: Ladies. Excuse me.

AXIS: I'd be on the red, you've got a nice shot there.

GUEST: 'Your shoots are an orchard of pomegranates
>   With all choicest fruits.'
>
> When I was at school a man stood up for a lady, and women did not play billiards.

THEENIE: I can't concentrate.

AXIS: Ignore him.

>   THEENIE *plays*.

Good shot.

THEENIE: It is lovely here. Cedar architraves, tinkling glass, moths in the velvet walls. I can't breathe.

AXIS: Stop worrying.

THEENIE: I want to rip up everything felt.

GUEST: She will ruin the cloth.
>   'You are stately as a palm tree
>   And your breasts are like its clusters.'
>
> [*Attempting to show* THEENIE *how to use the cue*] Madam, this is how you hold it.

AXIS: We got here first, thank you, sir. Get out.

GUEST: 'I say I will climb the palm tree
>   And lay hold of its branches.'

AXIS: Fuck off!

>   *The* GUEST *leaves*.

Wow! Did you see that?

THEENIE: Kiss me again. Come up to our room … Axis.

AXIS: Alabastar's with us and it's fine.

THEENIE: Why do they want to take him away from me?

AXIS: They're scared of me and you together.

THEENIE: They don't understand it.

AXIS: They can't control it. Alabastar has to turn out perfect or their empire falls in ruins. You have to work out whose life you're living. They'd force that child on you if they could split us up.

THEENIE: Don't say that. If I'm not holding onto you, nothing's real, nothing's safe.

AXIS: I can't be you. I want to finish the game.

THEENIE: I'll go.

>   Out. Up and down
>   This cold haunted town.
>   Run out and play baddies
>   Rape girls and old ladies,
>   Make havoc; why can't I?
>   I'm unnatural, aren't I?
>   If men can't have me, or my lover
>   They'll build a court and damn me,
>   Morally unfit to be a mother.

AXIS: Don't let politics leave you without a corner for yourself, or for me.

THEENIE: They're going to sue me.

AXIS: Oh shit, Theenie. This was supposed to be our decadent weekend away. If it didn't rain all the time in these painful mountains we could go out.

THEENIE: Alabastar doesn't want to go bushwalking.

AXIS: Alabastar? Alabastar! He's the only one enjoying this. Ice-creams at Echo Point, rides on the Scenic Railway.

> 'Knock knock …
> Who's there?
> Walter.
> Walter who?
> Wall to wall carpet …'

Chocolates at the Paragon Cafe and here, beside the log fire, in this stunning old camp hotel, Space Invaders.

> *Pinball machines.*

You gotta smile. He's winning enough free games to flog them off to the other kids. With a bit of luck he'll get up to paying the hotel bill.

THEENIE: You don't like him, do you?

AXIS: I don't want to be torn to pieces. I'll support you if you have to fight for him, but right now I've got to have some space for myself.

THEENIE: You want me to lose him. Go on, admit it, you want his father to get him.

AXIS: Don't be crazy.

THEENIE: You wish he didn't exist.

   AXIS *moves to leave.*

THEENIE: Axis, where are you going? Where are you going?
AXIS: Out.

   She leaves.

THEENIE: Let me come with you. [*Calling*] Alabastar!

   Pause.

 Axis! Wait! It's raining. Please.

   No answer.

 Alabastar, get your raincoat. We're going out to hug a gumtree.

   She leaves. Blackout.

SCENE SIX

KURT *and* MIRIAM'*s house.* MIRIAM *enters with a new baby wrapped in a shawl of purple, white and green, the suffragette colours.*

MIRIAM: [*sing*ing] I have a dolly
   With eyes of blue
   And hair that's curly brown.
   She wakes whenever I pick her up.
   And she sleeps
   When I lay her down.

   KURT *enters with a towel. Doing his morning exercises. His push-ups perform his dream of taking sexual possession of Axis.*

KURT: 'My head is wet with dew,
   My locks with the drops of the night.'
Why am I the one to have a dream about Axis? I'm too busy. But someone has to lie her down and do it. That way she would learn. Someone has to make the world safe. She'll have my sister—do you know how close I was to my sister? — parade around the court, demanding rights. Rights! The filthy, sanctimonious, demonstrating lesos.

MIRIAM: [*referring to the baby*] She looks like you, darling. Don't you think?
KURT: Of course, sweetheart. But she's got your chin, God help her.

Pause.

My colleagues trust me. Damn it! I won't have my reputation diminished by deviants dragging my sister into their clitoral insurgency.
MIRIAM: Don't swear, Kurt, she'll hear you.
KURT: Daddy's ittie girl. Sleeping.
'Your eyes are doves
Behind your veil.'
I'm not going to let Alabastar down.
MIRIAM: Little fingers curled like warm shells.
KURT: 'Round and round the garden
Chased the teddy bear …'
When he gets in his bookcase, Sylvester might look like a Marxist but he and Louise are thoroughly decent people.
MIRIAM: I know, I know, Louise is perfect. But can't you worry about them some other time? A baby is forever, yet, when you have one, it only lasts a little while.
'Rock a-bye baby
In the tree top …'
KURT: Will you ring Theenie up? See if she can be reasonable. Tell her it's in the boy's best interests if she hands him over quietly without the messy business of a court case.
MIRIAM: '… When the wind blows …'
KURT: I've got it! Invite her to the christening.
MIRIAM: She has to be there, silly, she's the star performer.
'… The cradle will rock …'
Look, she's smiling.
KURT: Darling, at that age it's wind.

He sighs.

I'm discussing Theenie, Auntie perilous Theenie.
MIRIAM: Theen and Axis sent this hand-crocheted shawl. And don't you swear. Feel how soft it is.

The shawl drops open to reveal a women's symbol worked into the cloth.

KURT: Good God, look at it. I warned you. The moment you have anything to do with them, they start hostilities.

MIRIAM: You forget, they grow so fast, this milk-warm baby smell.

KURT: Nothing matters to you, does it? Can you take time out to listen to me, Miriam? Freedom has to be fought for, it's very fragile. A red flag—

MIRIAM: 'It's very fragile. A red flag waver can come and break it, like that.'

She waves a squeaky toy in front of the baby.

Look, there's Daddy. Daddy!

KURT: Don't mock me, dear. Give me that.

He grabs the toy.

Do you think I'm working day and night simply for what you and I can get out of it?

MIRIAM: Don't you raise your voice at me, Kurt, I'm a nursing mother.

KURT: If I didn't care about Australia, I'd have sold out years ago. We could have bought an island in the South Pacific for a song and let this country go to the bitches.

MIRIAM: You're frightening her.

KURT: [*taking the baby*] There!

MIRIAM: Careful, Kurt.

KURT: I'll be careful.

MIRIAM: Careful. Don't you have to go in to work?

KURT: Miriam. There are moments when I almost wish I was you. I could forget about everything. Oh Gawd. [*To the baby*] Are you puking? All right. I'm sorry. I'll fix it. Where do you keep the cloth?

MIRIAM: Baby! [*Taking the baby*] If you knew how it makes me tired.

KURT: How it makes you tired!

MIRIAM: [*as she leaves, singing*] 'When the bough breaks
    The cradle will fall,

And down will come baby,
Cradle and all.'

KURT *changes lights with a karate gesture and leaves.*

SCENE SEVEN

Back at the hotel. AXIS *enters.*

AXIS: Where is she? It's nearly dark. She wanted me to hold her and I had to run away.

   VANDELOPE *enters with a billiard cue.*

Where is she?

VANDELOPE: I bet she's at the Paragon, knocking herself off with scones, jam and cream.

   She plays billiards.

AXIS: Vandelope, we just came from there. What if they wandered off the track?

VANDELOPE: She's probably stopped somewhere to do a rock carving. So much for your decadent weekend.

AXIS: She was driving me round the twist. 'We need to get away', I say, 'of course Alabastar can come'—there's no escaping kids—and she accuses me of hating him.

VANDELOPE: She's gotta put that Alabastar in a big basket and dump it on his dad's doorstep.

AXIS: He's not a bloody cross-eyed kitten.

VANDELOPE: Sylvester can cope. Their house is air-conditioned.

AXIS: Vandelope, it's taken me a while, but when you live in a house with a kid, their friends come and visit, they talk to you, and you get fond of them.

VANDELOPE: It's your go. Axis, love, you're holding it like a toothpick.

   AXIS *plays.*

AXIS: The table won't keep still. She knows the bush, I know she knows the bush.

VANDELOPE: This isn't a game, it's a nervous breakdown.

AXIS: Last week she ripped the knife through her big canvas; that's why we came up here.
VANDELOPE: I can see it's bad; it's in your eyes.
AXIS: Why can't she see that?
VANDELOPE: Have you given her the chance?
AXIS: We hardly see each other anymore. I'm either at the clinic or barmaiding. If we have to go through the courts to keep the kid, there'll be all those illegal fees, thousands. Theenie doesn't realise. I feel like I'll get punished whatever I do.
VANDELOPE: [*holding* AXIS] There's the world out there to get angry with and we keep turning the knives on ourselves.
THEENIE: [*off*] You'd better run upstairs, Alabastar, and get some dry clothes.
VANDELOPE: Wouldn't you know it? Right on dinner time.

  THEENIE *enters.*

THEENIE: I thought you'd caught the train.
AXIS: I haven't, have I?

  AXIS *and* THEENIE *embrace.*

VANDELOPE: Well, you didn't think I'd let you two bust up, did you?
AXIS: Hours. Hours and hours.
THEENIE: The wattle was in flower.
VANDELOPE: Well, I come up to the mountains for fresh air and a cappuccino, and there's Axis, staring into her cup of froth at the Paragon—Well, that was a fortuitous conjunction of the charts, wasn't it? Half the ghetto turns up, into the waffles, polishing off with a little bushwalk round the cliffs.
THEENIE: We saw the lyrebird.
AXIS: Did you?
THEENIE: She came out of the bush in front of us …
VANDELOPE: Some people have all the fun.
THEENIE: She fluffed her wings like an old woman gathering her skirts and ran, ran on her skinny legs down the track and disappeared.
AXIS: I wish I'd been there.

THEENIE: So do I. I was okay in the bush. I walk out of the tree ferns and the world's still everywhere.

VANDELOPE: I'm going to put my butt in, even if it gives you the shits. It doesn't matter where he lives from now on.

THEENIE: Don't you start driving me mad.

She turns to go.

AXIS: Come back. Theenie. We've got to work it out.

VANDELOPE: Let me finish. Theenie, they'll stick the kid in an old school tie, keep his vowels open, and try and teach him to despise us. But he won't turn out like them. He's been with you, he's got your sensitive world with him in here—

She indicates her head.

—And in here—

Her heart.

—And he's missed out on one or two of the cockfights that usually come with the balls.

THEENIE: You mean he's not a macho pig after all, and I still have to give him up?

VANDELOPE: But it's safe to let go of him; he doesn't throw beer cans at lyrebirds. Sure, he'll love life with the upwardly mobile, until he realises he has to swap honesty for knives and forks.

AXIS: He'll tell them where to stick it. And when he's older, he'll rebel and marry a feminist.

VANDELOPE: With a bit of luck he'll just live with him.

THEENIE: I don't care what fancy reasons you think up and I don't care if he grows cloven hoofs as well as a tail, he's my kid.

VANDELOPE: I know it's hard, but are you and Axis going to ruin your lives and alienate your friends just to save Alabastar from the nuclear family?

THEENIE: I love him and I'll be as emotional and irrational as I like, and I won't let anyone take him away, whether they attack from the right, or they attack from the left. And everyone screaming at me, 'It's for your own good, you understand, and we're sure it's in the best interests of the child.'

She leaves.

AXIS: How come a touch of honest feminism goes down like poison?

VANDELOPE: I meant it as an antidote. Run after her, tell her I didn't understand she was struck on him. Tell her I'll help. We'll raise the money and fight.

AXIS: Thanks. Wish me luck.

She leaves.

VANDELOPE: We could do with a good campaign. We're down on morale.

She leaves.

END OF ACT ONE

ACT TWO

SCENE ONE

Lights dim. A street very late at night outside SYLVESTER'*s house. 'LESBIAN M' has been painted on the wall. Car passing close. Headlights sweep by.* VANDELOPE *and* AXIS *hide. They have a torch, and* AXIS *has a pot of paint and a brush.*

VANDELOPE: They've gone.
AXIS: A taxi, fuck it. He'll have a radio.
VANDELOPE: Did he see us?
AXIS: Dunno. Got three more letters.

> AXIS *paints on the wall by torchlight: 'UMS'. Sounds of a police siren, car.*

VANDELOPE: Pigs! We can get through those bushes and over the fence.
AXIS: They've got a sausage dog called Yappy.
VANDELOPE: They would have.

> VANDELOPE *and* AXIS *hide.*

SERGEANT: [*off*] Mongrels!

> *Dog barks. The car drives away. Siren fades. Street lights on* AXIS *and* VANDELOPE. *They give one another a victory sign and a hug.*

VANDELOPE: [*shining her torch on the graffiti*] You little ripper.

> VANDELOPE *and* AXIS *exit.*

SCENE TWO

Daylight outside SYLVESTER *and* LOUISE'*s house. The graffiti on the wall is now visible: 'LESBIAN MUMS'.* SYLVESTER *and* KURT *enter.*

SYLVESTER: [*indicating the graffiti*] There.

KURT: Barbarians! On your own property. I've rung the papers. If she's forcing this case to court you'll need evidence of this infantile smearing.

SYLVESTER: Will you give me a moment to think? There has to be a rational way to give Alabastar the stability he needs. How did Theenie get mixed up in this idiotic extremism? We used to sit up for hours talking philosophy. Well, she's not going to make me guilty because I earn enough to buy this house. Alabastar likes it here. He's my son and I want him here, he's a great little person.

KURT: Inform her officially you're not sending Alabastar back, and if she doesn't call off this … war, you'll inform her employer she's a lesbian.

SYLVESTER: She's freelance. Your publicity will double the price of her paintings.

KURT: Freelance! You can establish in court that she doesn't have a steady income.

SYLVESTER: Will you lay off?

KURT: I've got it. Does Axis work? Get onto her boss. The top man.

SYLVESTER: She works at the Women's Clinic.

KURT: How promiscuous are they? You can prove it isn't a stable relationship.

    Pause.

Family! That's it. Say you'll spill the beans. The impenetrable Axis must have a mother and a father.

SYLVESTER: My God. Can't you base your arguments on a modicum of good taste?

KURT: Don't shrug your self-righteous shoulders at me, Syl old boy, I didn't scribble on your wall.

    LOUISE *enters with a tray of coffee things.*

KURT: Ah, Louise.
    'Let me hear your voice,
    For your voice is sweet
    And your face is comely.'

LOUISE: Why, Kurt! You're such a funny, gallant man.
KURT: The age of chivalry is not dead, and is that the flower of pregnancy blooming on your cheeks?
LOUISE: Oh, you! Lucky you and Miriam.
KURT: [*offering* LOUISE *a chair*] I am at your service any time.

Kisses her hand.

'O that you would kiss me
With the kisses of your mouth!
For your love is better than wine.'

LOUISE *pours coffee:*

LOUISE: Milk?
KURT: I'll have my women white, and my coffee black.
SYLVESTER: Let's have some semblance of respect for humanity.
KURT: Haven't you married delectable milk-white skin? Humanity will lose you Alabastar.
SYLVESTER: God knows why I ever let you interfere in what was a very convenient arrangement between Theenie and myself.
LOUISE: Dearest love, that wasn't working, you said that yourself—a month here with us, a month in that commune, the poor boy didn't know whether he was Arthur or Martha. He's nearly a teenager, he needs a routine. And look at our house. Just when the sauna arrives, she attacks us.
SYLVESTER: You don't think, darling, we provoked her, by keeping him here. It is her month.
LOUISE: Suppose I walk over here and stand in her shoes and there's her precious Alabastar on the other side of the wall. It looks like we kidnapped him. So she turns us into capitalist monsters whose house should be ruined. He wants to stay here. I thought we were doing the best we could for him sending him to Bedlingham Grammar, but if she thinks he's going to be happy mucking around way below his ability in an ordinary state school for the sake of her revolutionary principles, then I give up. I'm sorry. He needs the guidance. Violin and homework, and then he can play pinball.
KURT: Play! He should be making them.
SYLVESTER: You have overdrawn my patience.

KURT: That's where we're steering Matthew—computers.
LOUISE: Alabastar's artistic. Can't you see him in the Senate?
SYLVESTER: I wish I could give Alabastar life on a Mozart record. He was asking this morning when he was going to see his other mother—both of them. I want him to be happy, but so in her own strange way does Theenie.
LOUISE: Well, you'll be pleased to know we had a phone call from the Undone Graffiti Company. Don't look so worried. They specialise in sandstock bricks.
SYLVESTER: Cross your fingers they get here ahead of the press.

He leaves, taking the coffee tray.

KURT: 'O fairest among women …'
You're the only woman I can talk to. Miriam won't listen. You can feel free to talk to me. I know you're worried and I want to help. He's your boy now. What's on your mind?
LOUISE: I'm doing everything I can for Sylvester.
KURT: Do you think he's descended into apathy, or downright complicity?
LOUISE: He's carrying an enormous burden.

> VANDELOPE *and* AXIS *enter disguised as workers from the Undone Graffiti Company.* AXIS *has a cleaning machine, and a concealed pot of paint and brush.* VANDELOPE *has a cassette player, with Greek music—loud. If desired,* AXIS *could be the cleaning machine itself, operated by* VANDELOPE *by remote control.*

Hooray. There's the wall, we want it all off, do you hear? All off, completely off, it's got to be totally off, clean.
VANDELOPE: Buenos noces, madame et m'sieur.

> *During the following* AXIS *paints another word on the wall: 'OK!'*

Santa Lucia. Tinafto portoleni agapi, sa gapo, volpone,
Ik ike ok
Waynee weedy winky
Amo amas amat
Hoki mai, wahine.

LOUISE: What?

VANDELOPE: Qu'ils mangent de la brioche.

LOUISE: Turn it off.

VANDELOPE: What you say, lady?

LOUISE: [*turning towards* AXIS] Turn it off.

VANDELOPE: Hey! Honi soit qui mal y pense. Sui mar a luciar lustro d'argento.

LOUISE: I don't speak Greek.

    AXIS *and* VANDELOPE *exchange a look.*

VANDELOPE: [*miming needing a hose*] Pshhh.

LOUISE: Oh, round the back.

VANDELOPE: No, no, lady, you don't understand. Pshhh.

LOUISE: Round the back.

VANDELOPE: Danke schoen lady. [*To* KURT] Guten Tag, Mettwurst.

    VANDELOPE *and* AXIS *leave.*

LOUISE: I don't think anybody understands.

KURT: You can trust me.

    'O my love, in the clefts of the rock—'

LOUISE: I'm not in the mood. It's the past. I haven't got a past. Not like Sylvester has. No child of my own. No great love to look back on. Apart from the curtains in the lounge room, I can't point to something and say, 'That's what I did'. As long as that boy is here, or there, or anywhere, Sylvester is tied to *her*.

    SYLVESTER *enters unseen by* KURT *and* LOUISE.

KURT: You just need to be reminded how beautiful you are.

LOUISE: No!

KURT: Sylvester needs you, and my nephew needs both of you. You can hold this family together. Otherwise Sylvester will dither away on his well-cleaned academic bum until Theenie has manipulated Alabastar into a suitable case for a lobotomy.

SYLVESTER: Get out of here. Now.

LOUISE: Darling!

    KURT *sees what has been added to the wall graffiti.*

KURT: More! See?

LOUISE: What? Oh, no, Sylvester!

KURT: The ratbags. Fraternise with them and you turn this country into a cesspit for subversives. Hey, you! Where are you taking the kid? They're kidnapping Alabastar. Harlots!

He runs off.

LOUISE: Sylvester, do something.
SYLVESTER: It's their month, darling.
LOUISE: I could shake you at a time like this.
SYLVESTER: Don't, darling. Don't make it harder than it already is.
LOUISE: I'm not. It's just the strain of not knowing where we are.
SYLVESTER: Bear with me. I need you, sweet one.
LOUISE: All right, darling. I'm sorry. What would you like for dinner, darling?

LOUISE *and* SYLVESTER *leave.*

SCENE THREE

KURT *arrives. He cues in organ music and lights for a stained-glass window. Moves the table.* MIRIAM *arrives with the baby in a christening robe.* MIRIAM *poses for a flash photo.* KURT *takes the baby.*

MIRIAM: Careful!
KURT: 'My dove, my perfect one, is only one,
　　　The darling of her mother,
　　　Flawless to her that bore her.'

KURT *and* MIRIAM *pose together for four photos.* VIOLET *and* ARCHIBALD *enter.*

ARCHIBALD: I trust Theenie is not bringing her life's companion, the misfit?
VIOLET: Shhh, Arch. We're in church. Hullo, Miriam.

KURT *gives* VIOLET *the baby. Photo flash of* VIOLET *and the baby.* VIOLET *hands the baby to* ARCHIBALD.

Careful!

Flash of ARCHIBALD *and the baby. The baby gets passed*

along the line to MIRIAM. *Photo flash of each change of holding the baby. Change of lights.*

What a lovely service! But a bit rushed, don't you think?

ARCHIBALD: Come and sit down, Miriam.

The baby cries. MIRIAM *finds a dummy.*

VIOLET: Miriam, not a dummy, that is naughty. You'll make her a smoker in later life!

KURT: 'We have a little daughter,
And she has no breasts.
What shall we do for our daughter
On the day when she is spoken for?'

KURT *leaves.*

ARCHIBALD: Miriam, my dear, the best thing I could do for her was to sign a pink slip of paper.

VIOLET: Now, dear, it ought to be banked, for when she wants to go to university.

MIRIAM: Oh, Archibald, you darling generous fairy godfather. Thank you! She's too little to tell you herself. [*Showing the baby the cheque*] Look!

ARCHIBALD: May she grow to have the delicate charm and modest demeanour of her mother. And her grandmother.

VIOLET: And this, Miriam, belonged to her great-great-grandmother. It's her diary, her poetry, and pressed flowers.

MIRIAM: Oh. A treasure. For my wittle Sleeping Beauty.

KURT *enters with a huge package.*

KURT: Roll up, ladies and gents. Here in this tent we have the world's most proud, most lavish daddy. Guilty, ladies and gentlemen, of bringing you from the seven corners of the globe, the world's biggest, quadraphonic, walk-in, battery-operated—young Matthew can show her the wiring—*dolls' house.*

He opens the box away from the audience. The baby cries.

VIOLET: Careful, Kurt, careful.

KURT *takes the baby.*

KURT: For Daddy's noo girl? Can Sarah play too? If you can learn to stack the dishwasher half as quickly as your big sister Sarah, Daddy will be proud of you.

The baby cries. VIOLET *takes the baby. The crying stops.*

VIOLET: He earns at the bar more money than sense. And she ought to be feeding her baby now.

KURT: Well, darling, what does my favourite wife think of it?

MIRIAM: It's very, very … everything. How will she manage? It makes me want to crawl in there and hide.

KURT: Have you lost your contact lenses, woman? Don't thank me, will you?

MIRIAM: I was going to thank you, Kurt, of course I was.

KURT: No, just don't thank me.

MIRIAM: Baby.

She takes the baby.

'This little piggy went to market,
this little piggy stayed home …'

THEENIE *and* AXIS *enter.*

ARCHIBALD: Good afternoon, ladies.

THEENIE: Hullo.

VIOLET: Hullo, darling, hullo, Axis.

KURT: That settles it. Theenie, there is no basis for negotiation if you bring into my house, that—that … black witch.

ARCHIBALD: Son, will you have the intelligence to meet a crisis with the dignity of a gentleman?

AXIS: Oh double bubble, I forgot the cauldron. Can I have a hold of her?

KURT: No!

MIRIAM: I don't think I should let you.

VIOLET: [*to* AXIS] Keep your hand under her head.

She takes the baby from MIRIAM *and gives her to* AXIS.

AXIS: [*singing*] A caterpillar on a tree
Found a leaf to eat for tea.
Humpity humpity hump.
One day she felt the strangest things

Her body was growing legs and wings.
Humpity humpity hump.
She stretched herself, and climbed up high,
Bumpity bumpity bump
Left the branch and learnt to fly.
Humpity humpity hump.

KURT: Father, they're already turning Alabastar into a fairy. And we allow ourselves to be intimidated while she casts spells on my daughter. Look.

ARCHIBALD: Enough. I will speak to Theenie.

VIOLET: Come along, Miriam dear. I'll get you your cuppa, and you can feed her.

ARCHIBALD: Subtlety is more valuable than kingdoms.

AXIS: Alabastar can come too. He wants to see the baby.

THEENIE: Thanks, Axis.

AXIS: Courage! There's a full moon. Look at her funny baby nose.

VIOLET and AXIS, with the baby, go out.

KURT: Run after them, go on, save your baby.

MIRIAM: Oooh!

She leaves.

THEENIE: I want to ask you to stop insulting Axis. And me.

ARCHIBALD: You're very precious to me, Theenie. What's in the parcel?

THEENIE: It's a book.

KURT: The complete works of Ima Crank.

THEENIE: The pages are blank.

ARCHIBALD: For photographs.

THEENIE: Or drawings, paintings. One day she might write in it herself.

She gives the parcel to KURT.

KURT: I can see returning the helpful sister I remember.

ARCHIBALD: We all know and love a very attractive and intelligent Theenie.

KURT: We used to share our toys, remember; you loved marbles. I don't like to see you seduced into something that isn't you.

ARCHIBALD: I appreciate, my dear, the enormity of the sacrifice that has to be made, but I feel certain that the young lady, out of decency and loyalty towards you, will understand that you care too deeply for Alabastar to let him be taken away.

KURT: Think what it would mean to me personally, and to the whole family, if you left the proselytising to the frustrated fanatics and returned to being yourself.

ARCHIBALD: Of course, come over to us for as long as you need. Your mother will be delighted.

KURT: Miriam'll love to take you shopping, we'll arrange introductions, gallery openings …

ARCHIBALD: Kurt, we could convert your old room to a studio for her. And as for Alabastar's school fees, he shall have his share now while we're still alive.

THEENIE: No, thank you.

Pause.

KURT: Did I hear you?

Pause.

ARCHIBALD: It would behove you to explain, my dear daughter.

THEENIE: There's nothing I can say. Nothing.

ARCHIBALD: Nothing will come of nothing. Speak again.

THEENIE: I could paint the willow trees, the pretty willows hanging in the garden, I could eat steak and jacket potatoes with sour cream and chives. I could lie still at night with my curtains open and watch the moon make my bed cold. I could paint a branch hanging in the garden. I could wash and iron and put away my thoughts and my dreams until strength became my wardrobe door and all my joy its mothballs.

KURT: You're mad.

THEENIE: We'll sit at Sunday lunch and talk of veins in leaves and lineages, make kind, safe touches of the brush, and when I've learnt to sit there, silent, soft, false and vulnerable, like the tub of table margarine, you will nod your satisfaction, 'She is good enough for Alabastar'.

KURT: Every word she plunges deeper.

ARCHIBALD: My sometime daughter. I wipe my hands.

KURT *and* ARCHIBALD *leave.* MIRIAM *enters.*

MIRIAM: Oh, there you are. Thank you for the empty book.

THEENIE: Help me. Please. What Axis and I do isn't going to hurt Alabastar. Please tell Kurt.

MIRIAM: You make everything so difficult! You have to come in to lunch.

THEENIE: Wait. Who's going to tell Alabastar I can't see him any more?

MIRIAM: There's too much danger that he'll grow up a …

THEENIE: Yes, he will grow up. And as for the other unmentionable, he might. Or he might not. I don't know why Kurt's so scared of it—tell him it's free enterprise.

MIRIAM: Actually, I quite like Alabastar. He offered to babysit if I ever wanted to go to a meeting, but I do most of our entertaining here.

THEENIE: Tell him Alabastar can't be cut in half.

MIRIAM: What makes you think Kurt would listen to me? If I agreed with you … which I can't.

THEENIE: Ask him to drop the case or he can't screw you.

MIRIAM: I've just had a baby.

THEENIE: Suppose he was trying to take your baby away from you.

MIRIAM: He might, if I behaved like you.

She leaves.

THEENIE: Miriam!

Pause.

Axis, come and find me. I don't want to go on being an idealist. I keep getting disappointed.
 I paint split-second canvasses.
 In my head the walls come down.
 I hang a picture here,
 Violet, purple, lavender,
 Different, and not punished.
 This arms race ends,
 Power and all its weapons rot—

And boldly from the compost
Grow celery and walnuts.

VIOLET enters with a photo album.

VIOLET: The way you adults behave, you're worse than the children. You're shouting this whole house and family to pieces. Kurt, don't you raise your hand to her. Stop him, Arch! Where's your father, he needs his cup of tea.

She sees THEENIE.

Theenie, it's not good for you to be sitting in the draught, dear. There aren't enough hours in the day to be miserable, dear. If only you'd given Alabastar a little brother or sister while there was still time. I go inside my head and make up stories. You've got a minute, haven't you?

She opens the album.

THEENIE: It's nice, Mum. Do you know where Alabastar is? Violet, have you seen Alabastar and Axis?

VIOLET: What, darling? In this one you were—you would have been six, that's your big brother, Kurt, he'll be seven and a half, we like our picnic by the paperbarks. Now what have I done with it? Always losing things, your silly mother. Theenie? Have you got it? Have you got it? The bag of bread to feed the ducks?

THEENIE: Mum. This is now. I'm grown up. Don't go mad. You're cold.

VIOLET: It doesn't matter what the weather's like, dear, as long as you wear your warm singlet and don't sit on the concrete.

THEENIE: Will I get you a rug?

VIOLET: My helpful little Gappy.

THEENIE: This is not happening.

VIOLET: Don't you go worrying about me. Look at you. You'll get your two front teeth for Christmas, but you must put your paints away now and have your bath, your father's coming home, I've only got one pair of hands.

THEENIE: What have we done? Where are we? That's more than twenty years ago.

VIOLET: You mustn't cry, my darling daughter, you know I'm never unhappy. Brush your hair and it will shine like gold. Your father knows. He's bringing you home another box of paper. I've got all your paintings, safe and sound. Oh no, he has to load the rubbish on the trailer for the tip. 'If you can keep your head when all about are losing theirs …'

    AXIS *enters*.

AXIS: They've taken Alabastar. The fucking shits have taken Alabastar.

VIOLET: There she is. Stop shouting. Everybody's shouting.

AXIS: You've got to tell them all to get stuffed.

THEENIE: I can't.

VIOLET: I've got too much to do to sit here all day. There's only one thing that worries me, and that's when you children fight, it's the bane of my existence.

    She cries.

THEENIE: Mother, we won't fight any more.

AXIS: I'm sorry she's upset, but so am I.

THEENIE: Shhh!

AXIS: Will you listen to me. You've got to stand up to them, or they'll suck you in until you've gone as mad as the rest of them.

THEENIE: I told them what I wanted. I told Kurt. I told Dad. Whatever I do, I—

VIOLET: You can't go on shouting at your party.

AXIS: You're never going to satisfy them.

THEENIE: Where's Alabastar? He didn't come and say goodbye.

AXIS: He ran out to their car. With all the kids. Louise came and said they'd go disco-skating.

THEENIE: Why didn't you call me?

AXIS: I was screaming for you, this house is huge and fucking soundproof. I tried to run after Albie, Kurt grabbed my arms, I kicked him, we've got to get out of here.

    THEENIE, *crying, wipes her nose on her sleeve.*

VIOLET: Go and get a handkerchief, a sleeve is a sleeve.

THEENIE: Mum.
VIOLET: No, you don't have to hold onto me, it's a beautiful moon for a new baby. Where's your father, he needs his cup of tea. My strength is as the strength of ten, because my heart is pure.

She leaves.

THEENIE: I'll get her to lie down and sleep.

AXIS *stops her going.*

AXIS: Your father's there.
THEENIE: When she wakes up tomorrow, the world might have gotten better.
AXIS: Come back. You can't live her life.
THEENIE: When I look at the back of my hand I see my mother's, how it looked when I was small, and when I look in her face, it's too late. I love her. The only mirrors here are pinball screens. Help me. I want to find a picture of myself.

AXIS *hugs her.*

I shouldn't have brought you here, it's so sad.
AXIS: What about you?
THEENIE: You know how the raindrops hang in the morning on a blade of grass? She used to look for beauty, very early, before we kids woke up, and Dad wanted marmalade. I'd find her in the garden with her hands folded, breathing the sunrise, and the sparrows. She was patient for years and years, and now Kurt and I are fighting and they've taken Alabastar.
AXIS: You're living in this dreamworld. It drives me crazy. You've got to act, Theenie. In the court.
THEENIE: How can I fight them? I could if prejudice was a dragon and I didn't know its name. But it's not. It's my family.
AXIS: That doesn't mean you've got to give up yourself. They might learn something if they hear you being honest, out loud.
THEENIE: Not in public. I can't.

Pause.

Mum used to like what I painted.
AXIS: *You've* got to like it. You. I'm sick of our silence, Theenie. There's a lot of people supporting you, you know. If it has to

go to court, they'll be ready, really fast. We'll have a paste-up, leaflets, money coming in, a big demo, a bail fund, a dance at Balmain Town Hall.

THEENIE: You're scaring me shitless.

AXIS: Smile. Come on. Vandelope's out there raffling a few deals.

THEENIE laughs.

THEENIE: I'll have an exhibition. 'For Axis, who wouldn't let me give up.' We'll get Albie back. You're wonderful.

AXIS: That's the good news.

She takes out a letter.

Louise brought an agreement for you to sign. [*Reading*] 'To obviate the stress of a court case with its concomitant emotional and financial embarrassment, agreement must be reached for Alabastar to continue at Bedlingham Grammar School …'

THEENIE: Axis, we'll accept it. It's only a stuck up school, we can go back to month and month about, we can have our turn.

AXIS: I thought you were ready to fight.

She gives THEENIE the letter.

There's more.

THEENIE: [*reading*] He grants me access, one weekend in five, the Easter Break from the morning of Good Friday until Children's Day is over at the Show. And three weeks at Christmas, with alternating Christmas Days. All, Sylvester, is that all? Do we have to go down on our knees and beg for scraps of candles?

AXIS: That's not all God wants. Read the rest.

THEENIE: [*reading*] 'I undertake during any period of access to refrain from any word or act which may reasonably be calculated to suggest to Alabastar that I am, or any friend of mine is, a lesbian, such acts to include remaining overnight with any lover, or engaging in any public display of affection.'

She screams.

You kiss me back to life and then they kill me for it.

SCENE FOUR

The court. AXIS *and* THEENIE *watch as* SOLOMON *enters in the robes of a judge, with books, gavel, concealed flask of brandy.* VANDELOPE *enters with leaflets, collection bucket, books and papers ready to demonstrate against him.* SOLOMON *and* VANDELOPE *fight for control of the stage as they move the chairs and table into position.* SOLOMON *pushes* VANDELOPE'S *books onto the floor.*

VANDELOPE: [*giving the books and papers to* AXIS *and* THEENIE] Okay, sisters, hang in there.
SOLOMON: Out, vandal!
VANDELOPE: I'll be back. When you need me, yell.
SOLOMON: [*calling*] Constable!

> VANDELOPE *moves to leave, shouts, joined by crowd of demonstrators offstage.*

VANDELOPE: You're in there for us.
 We're out here for you.

> *She leaves. Demonstrators offstage, singing, chanting, shouting.*

SOLOMON: 'King Solomon excelled all
 The kings of the earth
 In riches and in wisdom.'
VANDELOPE & CROWD: [*off, singing*] We own our own bodies,
 We shall not be moved.
SOLOMON: 'And the whole earth sought
 The presence of Solomon
 To hear the wisdom which God had
 Put into his mind.'

> LOUISE *enters and takes up position in court.* AXIS *and* THEENIE *move to their positions opposite her.*

SOLOMON: Bring before me evil,
 Perverted and unnatural.
 Let it open and cavort—

We will sniff it out and kill it
In our Family Law Court.
VANDELOPE: [*off*] Not the church, not the state,
Women must decide their fate.
SOLOMON: As I apprehend we have here an application for custody, and the issue for me to try is whether or not in the pertaining circumstances account should be taken of the moral odium which attaches itself to homosexuals.
VANDELOPE: [*off*] Get your laws off our bodies.
SOLOMON: I am given to understand that a report has been entered by a Dr Gareth Porteus, Fellow of the Royal College of Psychiatry. [*Reading*] Homosexuality, in the literature, would seem to be something of an affliction, and while it may no longer be recognised as a criminal offence, or a disease, it is best avoided, especially in the young. Bring in the boy.
LOUISE: It's not the boy.
SOLOMON: Not the boy?
LOUISE: It's the mother, Your Honour.
SOLOMON: Impossible! Dear lady, ' ... you are going to tell the whole world that there is such an offence, to bring it to the notice of women who have never heard of it, never thought of it, never even dreamed of it. I think that this is a very great mischief ...' And there you have the very words of the Honourable Speaker of the House of Lords, London, nineteen twenty-one.
VANDELOPE: [*off*] Get your Lords off our bodies.
SOLOMON: The community in general is still sufficiently old-fashioned to view with disfavour, and even abhorrence, unnatural acts, whether between male and female, or male and male, or female and female, whether they be illegal or not.
THEENIE: [*offering reports and papers*] Your Honour, we have a report which counteracts ...
SOLOMON: The grave problem about all this is that I am already part heard on other matters and it is almost impossible for me to take up any extensive time with this matter; however, it is clear that some conclusion has to be reached on this matter if it is at all possible before lunch.

He consults his papers.

Summon the grandfather, Mr Archibald Havistock!

ARCHIBALD *enters.*

ARCHIBALD: Ask Alabastar what nine sevens are and he does not know. Ask him the capital of Tanganyika and he says, 'Can you lend me twenty cents?'

THEENIE: Look at him. His hair pressed onto his head, his tie, his neck held tight.

ARCHIBALD: From the Department of Education to the Gulag Archipelago we have spawned a generation who deny the distinction between good and evil.

THEENIE: His shoulders caught inside his suit, tight, tighter, his belly up against his belt, his shoes too narrow at the toes.

ARCHIBALD: To be modern is to stare at the destruction that flickers on the screen and have no way of knowing what it is.

THEENIE: He's frightened! He must hate it when the world around him seems to be coming undone.

ARCHIBALD: Bereft from a standard to tell him right from wrong, like a boy who has come to the end of his pile of coins, twentieth century man stands before posterity, disconnected and disappointed.

THEENIE: I can't bear it. Can't we find a paradise where your truth and mine can meet? You, whose love once held me on your knee.

SOLOMON: Order, order.

AXIS: After what we've been through, are you asking me to have sympathy for him?

THEENIE: Yes.

She cries.

ARCHIBALD: If the mother of my children were well and could be with us she would agree with me. Her voice was ever soft, gentle and low. I shall go from here, an old, tired man.

He leaves.

AXIS: [*concerned for* THEENIE] Adjournment, please, Your Honour!

SOLOMON: Five minutes!

He pulls out a small transistor radio and listens. The last few moments of a horse race. Meanwhile VANDELOPE *enters disguised as a doctor of laws, pours* AXIS *and* THEENIE *a cup of tea, dodges Solomon's view and adds a sign or graffiti: 'THE KOALA TEA OF MERCY IS NOT STRAINED'. She leaves.*

SOLOMON: 'Every one of them brought his present,
Articles of silver and gold,
Garments, myrrh, spices, horses and mules.'
That was the wrong bloody race! Time's up. Call the new wife.

LOUISE *moves forward.*

CROWD: [*off*] No god, no master … *No, No, Nanette*,
No god, no master … *No, No, Nanette*.

SOLOMON: Truly lovely.
'Our couch is green;
The beams of our house are cedar.'

LOUISE: Your Honour, we do not want Alabastar to despise his former mother. We would rather have protected him from the shock of learning she is … is …

SOLOMON: A lesbian?

AXIS: The bitch! How long are we going to sit here and put up with this?

LOUISE: It's not the way most people live. We love Alabastar very much. He's very happy with us. We've found him an excellent school, when time and weather permit we take him sailing, and his friends. We like children. But we're worried that if he goes on living in that commune, he'll be a teenager soon, he'll want to take a girlfriend home, she'll find out his mother's a … a …

SOLOMON: Thingamebob?

LOUISE: He'll be so … embarrassed.

THEENIE: Objection!

SOLOMON: Order!
'I adjure you, O daughters of Jerusalem,
That you stir not up nor awaken love

Until it please.'
LOUISE: Alabastar has expressed a wish to attend university, and we both encourage him in his studies. I do work part-time as my husband's research assistant, but I am always available to welcome Alabastar home from school, and his friends.
SOLOMON: A fair and far-sighted woman. Do you intend to have any children yourself with your current husband—out of curiosity, you understand?
LOUISE: Your Honour, well, at the moment, we are hoping. I'm not ... I'm not ...
SOLOMON: A lesbian. Thank you. Call the husband.

    SYLVESTER *enters.*

LOUISE: [*to* SYLVESTER] Stand up straight, darling, everybody's watching.
SYLVESTER: Your Honour, I am here reluctantly, without a bandwagon to push, or axes to grind. I remember with affection my former wife, and it is uncomfortable to be placed in opposition to her for the sake of a child we both love. Alabastar in his adolescence deserves a stable and consistent home with the love and role model of a father as well as a mother.
AXIS: [*to* THEENIE] Tell him we want a world without straitjackets.
THEENIE: Wait. I've got to understand what they want.
SYLVESTER: I respect his mother's right to her lifestyle *qua* lifestyle. That is her own choice. What causes me distress is her obsessive need to advertise what she is, to drag the drama past her bedroom door and seek public acclaim for a private idiosyncrasy.
AXIS: People get married on billboards!
SYLVESTER: In such a household, a household for the most part without men, I would feel afraid for Alabastar.
AXIS: If had a wart on my nose, and a cat, they'd burn us.
SOLOMON: Order! Words, words, as repetitive as muesli, Mahler, and our Asian future. Affidavits have been heard to the effect that in the first year of the boy Alabastar's life, the respondent wife had the eccentricity to hold an exhibition of paintings,

which provided entertainment to a heated crowd and a hot press …

AXIS: She made them look at things, and they hated it.

SOLOMON: … While the young husband, embarking on his career, had the burden of the child, and nobly filled the vacuuming.

THEENIE: Objection! Sylvester, tell them we shared the housework.

During the following dialogue between THEENIE, LOUISE *and* SYLVESTER, SOLOMON *swigs surreptitiously from his brandy flask.*

SYLVESTER: Objection, Your Honour.

LOUISE: You can't object to that, darling.

SYLVESTER: Christ, she's never neglected Alabastar. I was through my PhD by then, I could afford childcare, we helped one another. Christ, if I'd had her talent. If the press hadn't given her a ducking. Louise, I need your support and your love.

LOUISE: You're my life, Sylvester.

THEENIE: Louise! If you put yourself in a cage, how can any of us be free?

SYLVESTER: I've said from the beginning this case can't go through if it means assassinating Theenie. Darling, let's go home. Now. You and me. Us.

LOUISE: If we walk out of here without Alabastar, you'll never forgive me.

SYLVESTER: You're right. When he's with me I remember growing up. I'm not cut off from kangaroos and crazy things. And he's got those precious independent eyes. Theenie, I haven't any choice, we can't control this. Your Honour …

THEENIE: Sylvester, don't give him power over us.

SYLVESTER: Your Honour, objection withdrawn.

SOLOMON: *Ipso dipso*, the origins of the former wife's fractured family stem from the excesses of her artistic period.

CROWD: [*off*] What do we want?—Clear thinking.
   When do we want it?—Now.

SOLOMON: Who's next?

   AXIS *and* THEENIE *move forward.*

SOLOMON: 'Who is that coming up from the wilderness,
   Leaning upon her beloved?'
Two of them. Custody confers the responsibility of proper training and example. This factor of your alternative admitted lifestyle which is not the normally considered life of the majority, does not make you, *per se*, an unfit mother, but it cannot, in conscience, be ignored.

> SOLOMON *motions* THEENIE *to move back and* AXIS *to take a position ready for being questioned.*

SOLOMON: In your fragmented family, do you not think the boy Alabastar will be subjected to social discomfort? To the ridicule of his peers?
AXIS: Not unless you give them lessons.
SOLOMON: Young lady, be warned.
AXIS: 'Solomon had seven hundred wives, princesses,
   And three hundred concubines."
SOLOMON: What was that?
AXIS: Kings, chapter eleven, verse 3.
SOLOMON: The devil would quote the scriptures, eh? I could have you charged for contempt of court. Alabastar would be at a disadvantage, would he not, in that normal parents would not allow their sons to mix with known homosexuals.
AXIS: Especially if they had halitosis or were blacks.
SOLOMON: Ms Axis, are you not denying yourself your own instinct for motherhood, if we try to complete the picture of the odd situation you have there?
AXIS: Get your laws off my body.
SOLOMON: I could use this as a further opportunity to deplore the sort of exceedingly imprecise language which does nothing to assist the court. Do you attend clubs of the type where homosexuals congregate?
CROWD: [*off*] We want to be
   Nuclear free.
SOLOMON: Don't mumble. What goes on at these clubs? Do you see anything wrong in the boy seeing you, and you, unclothed, at a beach designated 'nude'? Have you no thoughts on an old fashioned virtue called modesty?

AXIS: None.
SOLOMON: If the boy were to entertain notions of homosexuality, would you not seek to dissuade him from these notions?
AXIS: Alabastar knows himself.
SOLOMON: Mmm. Ms Axis, in what role may we see you in relation to the child? A duplicate mother figure? A father figure?
AXIS: You can't fit me into your boxes. You haven't got one that's my size.
SOLOMON: You do not see anything wrong with yourself, do you?
AXIS: No!
SOLOMON: How many of these unnatural relationships have you had?
AXIS: I'm going to explode.
SOLOMON: Do you, how shall I put it, in whatever it is that the two of you do together, involve the child?
AXIS: We make billycarts together. You're the porn-pusher, not us.
SOLOMON: What is it exactly that you and you do together? Is there no danger of you leaving, in the bedroom or the bathroom where the child may come upon them, any sexual instruments that you may use?
THEENIE: Your Honour, our love is not a violent thing.
CROWD: [*off*] Free our bodies, free ourselves.
SOLOMON: You are of a religious, an evangelical nature, are you not?

Police siren.

AXIS: The pigs.
THEENIE: What if they're hurting people out there?
AXIS: Think of something.

THEENIE *grabs books and papers.*

THEENIE: We can produce evidence to refute the idea that homosexuality is linked with mental illness. Statistically lesbians are as well adjusted as their heterosexual counterparts, and in some cases may consume less valium. There is no evidence that homosexual households create homosexual children, any more than the other way round. Openness and acceptance of sexual diversity could contribute to a child's well-being and growth. There is clear statistical evidence that most sexual offences are committed by heterosexual men upon women, and not by lesbian women upon children.

AXIS: Put your hand up. See if he'll listen.

THEENIE: Sir!

SOLOMON: Yes, Theenie. You can be excused.

THEENIE: Sir! Could this case be considered not as a debate about sexual preference, but one about a world which does not trust and value women?

SOLOMON: You don't know what you're talking about. Out of order.

THEENIE: We've lost. I try to use their language, and still they refuse to understand.

> AXIS *and* THEENIE *hold one another.*

SOLOMON: Order! This perverse affection cannot be allowed. I have weighed most carefully what I have heard. The law is cognisant of current debate about the position of women. Women deserve the respect and freedom of an equal partnership with men, and no higher compliment can be paid her, than that she devote herself to the welfare of her family within that partnership, as an equal. Servile wombs cannot create free men. However, when radical forces attack the familiar way of joining people together, they attack the cement of our society. It is my melancholy duty to uphold the sanctity of womanhood against those who wish to profane it.

THEENIE: Mr Justice Solomon, this is not a criminal court. Why have I been on trial since I began?
> One child instead of two, guilty;
> Three legs on my studio easel, guilty;
> Four legs in bed and all of them gentle.
> Five dirty socks found in the cupboard, guilty.
> Six o'clock and it's not my turn for cooking, guilty;
> Seven days in the weakness—
> [*Singing*] Eight ladies dancing, guilty.
> Nine o'clock and he's up playing pinball, guilty;
> [*Singing*] There were ten in the bed
> And the little one said …

Write this in your books: She stood in the court and said, Let the women ask the questions.

She includes with a gesture herself, AXIS *and the women demonstrating outside the court.*

VANDELOPE & CROWD: [*off, singing*] Just like the trees that grow
> Until the forest sings
> We shall not be moved.

SOLOMON: Young lady, do you think a mere anyone can be initiated into the mysteries and ritual when it has taken us centuries to wrap the cloak around us? And you are merely a woman. After thorough deliberation the court awards the boy Alabastar to that dedicated family, man and wife, whose love, propriety and property will enable him to follow his chosen career, and to grow to manhood exercising responsibility for all that is worthwhile in our society.
'His legs are alabaster columns,
set upon bases of gold.'
Court dismissed.

He gathers his books to leave.

THEENIE: No, please no.

AXIS: [*calling*] Vandelope, help, ho!

CROWD: [*off, singing*] We own our own bodies
> We shall not be moved.

> VANDELOPE *enters as a doctor of laws, disguised as a man. Change of lights, puff of smoke to indicate fantasy.*

VANDELOPE: [*shakes hands with* SOLOMON] Dr Vandel Hope, QC. Give me leave to emulate your peroration.

SOLOMON: At last, a man after my own heart.

They sing and dance.

VANDELOPE & SOLOMON: You put your right hand in,
> You pull your right hand out,
> You put your right hand in,
> And you shake it all about.
> You do the hokey pokey
> And you turn around

And that's what it's all about.

SOLOMON: [*offering his flask*] Brandy?

VANDELOPE: Your Honour!

She drinks. Sound of the crowd, off, shouting.

SOLOMON: Attention those nincompoops attempting illegal entry by climbing through the skylight. You are endangering your own lives and you are endangering the lives of policemen.

He calls.

Constable! [*To* VANDELOPE] Lunch, as soon as the police clear through to the gate.

VANDELOPE: I have startling new evidence.

SOLOMON: [*checks his fob watch*] This is most irregular.

VANDELOPE: I would speak so the scroungers and riff-raff out there—listen and learn.

SOLOMON: Order. The court will come to order.

Noise of the crowd lessens.

VANDELOPE: Your Honour, it is the concern of this court that the boy grow up responsible, is it not?

SOLOMON: Let the rabble listen and be ashamed.

VANDELOPE: You would agree that every man is the maker of his own fortune?

SOLOMON: You put it neatly.

VANDELOPE: Then the boy must be able to make his own decisions.

SOLOMON: What? The boy?

VANDELOPE: All of us. Take control of our own lives. We could do it, in time, if there was no prejudice between us, and no power above us.

SOLOMON: Abandon the rule of the law?

VANDELOPE: You can retire, Your Honour.

SOLOMON: Puppy! People come to Solomon begging for wisdom.

VANDELOPE *takes a Bible off* SOLOMON'*s table and opens it.*

VANDELOPE: You would uphold the judgement of King Solomon?

SOLOMON: You mock me.

He pulls the Bible from VANDELOPE.

How can you, a doctor of laws, make a plaything of our finest precedent? You invite the jungle to take over and blood to flow in the streets.

VANDELOPE: You would stand by Solomon's ruling, no matter what?

SOLOMON: I have sworn it.

VANDELOPE: Have it your own way.

SOLOMON: Bring me a sword.

    SYLVESTER *hands him the sword.*

VANDELOPE: 'And they stood in awe of the King
Because they perceived
That the wisdom of God was in him
To render justice.'

SOLOMON: Have the women stand before me.

    LOUISE *and* THEENIE *come forward.*

'Divide the living child in two
And give half to the one
And half to the other.'

THEENIE: You can't cut Albie in half.

SOLOMON: [*indicating* THEENIE] The woman whose son was alive said to the king:
'Oh, my lord, give her the living child
And by no means slay it.'

THEENIE: At least let me go and hug him goodbye. I'll tell him. He's going to live with his dad for a while.

LOUISE: Alabastar will be very happy with us.

SOLOMON: [*indicating* LOUISE] The other said,
'It shall be neither mine nor yours:
Divide it.'

LOUISE: We've moved the Space Invaders into his room. Theenie can come and see him if she wants to. Sylvester?

SOLOMON: 'Then the king said,
Give the living child to the first woman
And by no means slay it;

She is its mother.'
The law allows it and the court awards it.
THEENIE: Did he say?
AXIS: Yes.
THEENIE: Hooray!

She hugs AXIS.

SOLOMON: What? The law awards the child to the natural mother, but this natural mother is unnatural. The law allows the ruin of the law?
VANDELOPE: [*removing disguise*] You swore it, Sol, old pal.
SOLOMON: [*his authority severely shaken*] You! You have spent hours obfuscating me. It has to be the other way round. There is too much at stake.
VANDELOPE: There's been fifty-eight people arrested; are you dropping the charges?
SOLOMON: Harlots! The law has to be cherished or you wreck the civilisation of centuries.

Pause.

[*Aside*] The words are coming out, why aren't they rousing … ?

He looks at VANDELOPE, AXIS *and* THEENIE.

Why aren't you frightened of the damage you will cause? Don't turn away from me. For my children's sakes I had an empire to hold onto and I cannot have you telling me it's gone. And yet, you remind me of my wife, of Miriam, when she used to get up in the morning and sing.

He leaves, defeated.

VANDELOPE: In real life it could be a bit more difficult.
LOUISE: Well, do we talk about it, or what?
THEENIE: I've never talked to you. I'm going to need some coffee.
SYLVESTER: He says he doesn't want to play pinball any more. He won thirteen free games in a row and after that there's nothing else to do. I love him, don't you see? I love him too.
AXIS: I could do with some champagne.
THEENIE: I want to paint, a circus.
VANDELOPE: The law keeps itself strong

PINBALL

Rewards those who make it,
Invents endless reasons
Why people should take it.
But you never know what
We could change
If we risk it.
Join hands friends
And we can go home
Optimistic.

THE END

www.ingramcontent.com/pod-product-compliance
Lightning Source LLC
Chambersburg PA
CBHW050023090426
42734CB00021B/3392